A Guide to North Carolina's Wineries

A Guide to North Carolina's Wineries

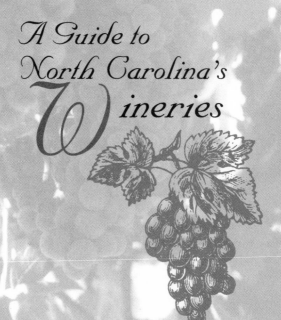

by
Joseph Mills and Danielle Tarmey

John F. Blair, Publisher   Winston-Salem, North Carolina

Published by John F. Blair, Publisher

*The paper in this book meets the guidelines
for permanence and durability of the
Committee on Production Guidelines*

UNLESS OTHERWISE NOTED,
ALL PHOTOGRAPHS ARE BY DANIELLE TARMEY

PHOTOGRAPHS ON FRONT COVER ARE OF
SHELTON VINEYARDS AND WESTBEND VINEYARDS

Library of Congress Cataloging-in-Publication Data

Mills, Joseph, 1965–
A guide to North Carolina's wineries / by Joseph Mills and Danielle
Tarmey.
p.   cm.
Includes bibliographical references and index.
ISBN 0-89587-268-4 (alk. paper)
1. Wineries—North Carolina—Guidebooks. 2. Wine and wine
making—North Carolina—Guidebooks. 3. North Carolina—Guidebooks. I. Tarmey, Danielle. II. Title.

TP557.M545 2003
641.2'2'09756—dc21
2002155554

DESIGN BY DEBRA LONG HAMPTON

Contents

Wineries of Eastern North Carolina

$\mathcal{P}$reface

In this book, we provide information about the North Carolina wine industry. We do not, however, evaluate, compare, or comment on wines. Some people like dry wines, and some like sweet ones. Some prefer Sauvignon Blanc, and some swear by Scuppernong. We have no interest in presenting our personal tastes as some kind of standard, but we do believe that even when people know their likes and dislikes, they should continue to try new and different wines. We agree with Larry Ehlers of Chateau Laurinda, who notes, "People will say, 'Well, I only drink California Merlot,' and I feel that's sad. There's a lot of other states besides that one. There's 49 other states you're missing. It's kind of like looking at one closet in the house and never going into any other rooms."

Here, we suggest what "rooms" are in North Carolina and give a brief history of each winery. Each has its own personality, and each has a story. This is why touring them is so interesting.

Because the industry changes rapidly, we urge people to call before visiting. Wine lists and tasting-room hours change. Some wineries hold special summer hours or close completely during the winter. Within the next few years, many new wineries will open and some, unfortunately, may close.

As we worked on this project, we discovered that the real pleasure of visiting wineries is talking to the people involved. They come from diverse backgrounds—art and accounting, teaching and textiles, science and social work—but they share a number of characteristics. People in the business tend to be stubborn, independent, strong-willed, opinionated, and unafraid to take risks. They also are forthright, hardworking, and optimistic. One winemaker admitted, "My wines sucked last year," then explained the intensive pruning program he had instituted. It required grueling hours in the vineyard, but he was convinced that it would make his wines better. In fact, we have never met a winemaker who wasn't striving to improve his or her wines and who wasn't absolutely convinced of future success in doing so.

We also found that most winery owners, winemakers, and vineyard managers are remarkably generous with their time and energy. They have a passion that they want to share with others. Perhaps this is why we go to wineries. We want to sample what's in the bottle, but we also want to catch a glimpse of the passion and the effort that put it there.

$\mathcal{A}$cknowledgments

We would like to thank all of the people
in the industry who shared their knowledge, experiences,
and enthusiasm with us. Without their generosity,
this guide could not have been written.
Special thanks is due LeRoy Percy, who first told us
about North Carolina wine.

Westbend Vineyards

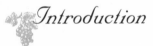

Introduction

For people interested in North Carolina wine, 2002 was a good year. Not only were winemakers excited about the harvests, but the state's wineries became easier to find. In 1999, the North Carolina legislature finally recognized that visits to wineries should be considered tourism. Three years later, the Department of Transportation began installing road signs to indicate their locations. From the Blue Ridge Mountains to the Atlantic Ocean, directional signs featuring a purple grape cluster began appearing on interstates and highways. As one winery owner noted, "Suddenly, people knew we were here."

Although it took decades for America's wine industry to recover from the "great national experiment" of Prohibition, it is now flourishing. Every state has at least one winery, and there are over a hundred "appellations," or American Viticultural Areas, that have been recognized as distinct grape-growing regions. Wine sales increase each year, and touring wineries has become a major recreational hobby. In North Carolina, for example, it is estimated that a million people visit wineries and vineyards annually.

Most of the growth in the North Carolina wine industry has occurred in the last 10 years. In 1991, the state had 68 commercial vineyards and a handful of bonded wineries. As of this writing, there are 22 wineries (with several more planning to open soon) and over 240 vineyards. Almost everyone involved in the business applauds this expansion. Stephen Lyons of Raffaldini Vineyards points out, "The absolute best thing to happen to a winery is to have another winery open right next to it. Then it becomes a destination." In certain parts of the state, people can now tour multiple wineries in a day. In the North Carolina Piedmont, for example, a half-dozen wineries are within 30 minutes of one another. In fact, in 2002 the Bureau of Alcohol, Tobacco and Firearms granted the Yadkin Valley appellation status because of its combination of soil and climate.

North Carolina wineries are diverse. They range from Biltmore Estate Winery, which produces over 100,000 cases a year and is the most-visited winery in America, to The Teensy Winery, which some years produces 300 gallons of wine and some years produces none at all. There are wineries located in old farmhouses, Quonset huts, basements, and newly constructed showpiece buildings. Visitors can look at art at the Germanton Vineyard and Winery or the Silver Coast Winery, play boccia at Waldensian Heritage Wines, or take in a dinner show at Duplin Wine Cellars.

The wines themselves are diverse as well. In fact, no other wine region in the world grows every major type of grape, including vinifera, French-American hybrids, labruscas, and muscadines. North Carolina offers wines for every taste, from sweet scuppernong to bone-dry Seyval Blanc. Many wineries also offer fruit wines, such as apple, blackberry, pear, and plum. At least two wineries make sparkling wines, and several are planning to offer port in the near future.

The increase in the number of wineries has been matched by an increase in the festivals that feature wines. These now include the Dobson Farm Festival, sponsored by Surry Community College in May; the North Carolina Wine Festival, held at Tanglewood Park near Winston-Salem in June; the Yadkin Valley Wine Festival, held in Elkin in June; the Pinehurst Labor Day Wine Festival; the Foothills Wine, Art, and Music Festival, held in Wilkesboro in October; the Seafood Festival, held in Morehead City in October; and the Southern Christmas Show, held in Charlotte in November. Attendance at these festivals has grown dramatically. In 2001, the North Carolina Wine Festival attracted 5,000 people. The following year, that number more than doubled, to 11,000. In addition to these general festivals, most wineries offer special events such as concerts, Fourth of July parties, and harvest celebrations. Not only can people taste wine and buy bottles at these festivals, but thanks to a legislative change, they can also purchase wine by the glass.

The industry's growth has altered the way some of the state's wineries operate. For example, to post a tourism sign on a highway, a winery must be open at least four days a week for 10 months of the year. Consequently, most wineries now have standardized hours (although you should still call ahead). With the increased interest and traffic, many wineries have implemented tasting-room fees. These usually range from three to five dollars, and they sometimes include a souvenir glass or are refunded with the purchase of a bottle. Almost every winery has a website, and many offer the opportunity to order wine on-line. At the moment, however, this option is limited to North Carolina residents. Currently, wine can be shipped among only 13 states—California, Colorado, Idaho, Illinois, Iowa, Maine, Minnesota, Missouri, New Mexico, Oregon, Washington, West Virginia, and Wisconsin—and even these have varying laws about the practice. North Carolina residents cannot ship wine from out of state, though they may personally transport up to 50 liters of table wine.

North Carolina wines have been earning distinctions in national and international competitions for years, but recognition of their quality has increased recently. The industry also has been aided by research studies that demonstrate the health benefits of wine. Whether they're working with Merlot or muscadine, everyone agrees that these are exciting times to be making wine in North Carolina. As Lillian Kroustalis of Westbend Vineyards says, "This is an industry whose time has come. It's happening, and it's going to happen."

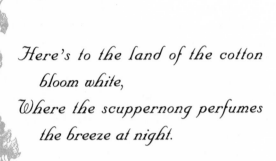

Here's to the land of the cotton bloom white,
Where the scuppernong perfumes the breeze at night.

Second verse of the
North Carolina state toast

The History of Wine in North Carolina

In 1900, North Carolina wines won medals at the Paris Exposition. It wasn't a fluke. Four years later at the Louisiana Purchase Exposition in St. Louis, a champagne from the state took the grand prize for sparkling wines against competition from other states, as well as France, Italy, and Argentina.

The maker of these medal winners was Paul Garrett, one of the most important figures in the history of American wine. Garrett built a business empire that spanned the nation. At one point, Paul Garrett & Co. was selling almost a million cases a year. His success owed as much to his flair for marketing as to the quality of his wines. In his promotional materials, he argued that wine should be considered a food, noted its medicinal properties, and insisted that if people drank wine regularly, it would "forever remove the vexatious problem of intemperance." Critical of those who insisted on drinking "foreign" wines, he emphasized both the heritage and patriotism of his products. For example, bottles of Garrett's American Wines prominently featured an eagle. His most popular brand, Virginia Dare, was named after the most famous woman of Roanoke's Lost Colony.

Garrett's advertising created an enduring North Carolina belief. The back of one pamphlet showed an old vine that Garrett claimed was "discovered in 1585" and was the source of the rootstock for many of the state's vineyards. This "Mother Vine" has become an important symbol for the state's wine industry, even though viticulture scholars such as Clarence Gohdes, author of the book *Scuppernong*, suggest the story is highly improbable.

The real history of North Carolina wine, however, is just as impressive as the one constructed by Garrett. It covers hundreds of years and consists of repeating cycles. Several times in the past two centuries, the industry has grown vigorously and then collapsed.

The first Europeans who came to the North Carolina area commented on the wild grapes they saw. The earliest known account is by Giovanni da Verrazano, who explored the coast in 1524 and wrote about the "many vines growing naturally there." He thought that "without doubt they would yield excellent wines." Sixty years later, colleagues of Sir Walter Raleigh described the coast of North Carolina as "so full of grapes that the very beating and surge of the sea overflowed them. They covered every shrub and climbed the tops of high cedars. In all the world, a similar abundance was not to be found." In fact, Gohdes notes, "legend has it that Sir Walter Raleigh took back to England 'a white grape that was esteemed among the best ever seen' and it was cultivated by Queen Elizabeth's patronage."

These wild grapes, varieties of muscadines that grow only in the American South, were made into wine by a number of colonists. In 1737, Irish physician John Brickell noted of North Carolina, "There are but few *Vineyards* planted in this Colony at present, for I have seen but one small one at Bath-Town and another at *Neus* [New Bern], of the White Grape, the same with the Madera. I have drank the Wine it produced, which was exceeding good." The 1878 *Guide Book of North-Western North Carolina* noted that "in 1769, three settlements of Carolina Moravians made nineteen hogsheads from 'the great abundance of wild grapes.' " By the first decades of the 19th century, thousands of gallons of wine were being made throughout the state, and scuppernongs were beginning to be cultivated as a crop.

The first important figure in the history of North Carolina wine was Sidney Weller, who established vineyards in Halifax and wrote two groundbreaking articles—"The Southern System of Vine Culture and Wine Making" in 1835 and "Wine Making, as Practiced in North Carolina" in 1845. Weller sold not only grapes and wine, but vine cuttings as well, and he systematically studied viticulture. He also invented a new trellising system. But his greatest influence was as a promoter, rather than a grower. He championed the scuppernong in every forum possible, believing that everyone should grow at least some of the grapes. In an 1832 article, he insisted, "If only as a pleasurable employment for hours of relaxation from business, attention to cultivation of vines would afford present compensation to a tasteful, virtuous mind. A number of vines, in regular order, is beautiful and agreeable to the sight especially in the season of leafing and bearing. Then becoming ripe, the Scuppernong and some other choice kinds of grapes, perfume the air around some distance with a delightful healthful fragrance. As an article of innocent luxury, no family of settled residence should dispense with rearing a few vines, at least." Weller's Vineyard eventually was renamed Medoc Vineyards. By 1840, it led the country in wine production.

Although many of those interested in making wine or having a vineyard first tried French vinifera, they had little success. In fact, Paul Lukacs points out in *American Vintage: The Rise of American Wine* that every colony planted vinifera, but no one could get the vines to survive. They were defenseless against pests and diseases to which native plants have a natural resistance. Consequently, farmers turned to scuppernongs. Easy to grow and flavorful, scuppernongs became known as the "Grape of Grapes" and "the Grape of the South."

Joseph Tongo, an enterprising viticulturist, chose North Carolina over Virginia and Kentucky because the land "flows with the milk of human kindness and Scuppernong wine." Intending to make Wilmington "the Bordeaux of America," he started the North Carolina Vine Dresser and Horticultural Model Practical School. In 1849, he advertised that students over 14 years of age would be taught "all the manipulations of the Vineyard, the orchard, and horticulture in general. The pupils will be taught besides all the practical and scientific details of grape and fruit raising &c, the art of making wine, and of taking care of it at all periods of ripening." The school was a failure, but the vineyard flourished.

The 1850s saw a national grape craze. During that time, North Carolina had at least 25 wineries and numerous vineyards. By the end of the decade, a doctor in Boston insisted that "with proper attention and care, Scuppernong wine may be made so fine as to excel all other wines made on this continent; and I would earnestly advise those interested to attend to the cultivation of this grape, in regions where the vine will grow, and make use of more skill in the manufacture."

The state's thriving industry was devastated, however, by the Civil War. David Fussell of Duplin Wine Cellars explains, "We were the leading wine state in the Union. When we seceded from the Union, the Southern winemakers no longer paid and maintained their federal bonded wine licenses. So when North Carolina lost, they were not licensed by the federal government to operate. Since North Carolina had dominated the wine market, like California is dominating it today, in the reconstruction of the South, the conquering forces decided that they didn't want us to make wine, so they would not renew these boys their federal wine licenses."

Eventually, the state's industry did rebuild. In fact, scuppernongs were championed as the best crop to grow because they required minimal labor. (Paul Garrett called a scuppernong vineyard "a literary man's Utopia and a lazy man's Paradise.") Farmers were encouraged to grow grapes as a solution to a depressed economy, and wine was seen as an important part of the future. By the end of the century, North Carolina was again at the forefront of the nation's industry. The Tryon area had a number of commercial vineyards. The Waldensian community in Valdese had brought a winemaking tradition with it from Europe. The federal government was heavily promoting scuppernong grapes, and Paul Garrett had begun building his empire.

Although the industry thrived for several decades, the state's temperance movement succeeded in crushing it yet again. In 1909, North Carolina enacted a statewide prohibition on alcohol. Garrett moved his business to Virginia. In 1917, he had to move again—this time to New York—when Virginia went dry. Then, in 1919, the 18th Amendment enacted Prohibition throughout the country. In *Winegrowing in Eastern America*, Lucie T. Morton notes, "The eastern wine industry was so effectively ruined by Prohibition and its aftermath that today the region's vineyards and estate wineries are objects of surprise and curiosity in areas where local wines were once taken for granted."

A straw poll conducted in 1932 indicated that two states wanted to continue Prohibition: Kansas and North Carolina. In the following decade, many counties throughout the state voted to return to being dry. Although during the Depression scuppernongs again were cited as a crop that would promote employment, it was decades before making wine reemerged as a serious commercial endeavor. As David Fussell puts it, "If you're slapped once, you may come back, but if you get slapped a couple times, you don't."

Paul Garrett managed to shepherd his company through Prohibition, in part by offering such products as Virginia Dare Tonic, a "medicament" with beef extract and pepsin, and Virginia Dare Flavoring Secrets, which included 21 flavors, such as fruit, peppermint, and vanilla. But in the 1930s, he couldn't convince Southern farmers to plant the grapes he needed to expand. By the time of his death in 1940, Virginia Dare Wine, which had been known for its scuppernong flavor, was no longer made with any of the grape.

In the 1950s and 1960s, the federal government promoted the growing of scuppernong grapes. Many farmers sold their crops to Northern wineries. A few wineries tried to establish themselves in North Carolina, but none lasted long. Lucie T. Morton explains, "The thirty five years from Repeal to the 1968 passage of the Pennsylvania Limited Winery bill was for the most part a 'dark ages' for American wine in general and for that of eastern America in particular."

Of North Carolina's current wineries, only two date back as far as the late 1970s: Duplin and Biltmore. By the early 1980s, these were joined by two more: Germanton Vineyard and Winery and Westbend Vineyards. These wineries did well until legislative changes in the mid-1980s again curtailed the industry.

Over the last 10 years, significant growth has occurred again. Not only are there hundreds of new vineyards, but a wide variety of grapes are being planted. After Biltmore and Westbend demonstrated that vinifera could be grown successfully in North Carolina, many followed their lead. In fact, in the 1990s, for the first time in the state's history, the acreage of planted vinifera exceeded that of scuppernongs. Now, once more, grapes are being championed as an important part of the state's economy.

In 1935, Paul Garrett hailed grapes as "a new money crop for the farmer." It's a description that sounds strikingly contemporary.

How do you make a small fortune in the wine business? Start with a large fortune and buy a winery.

A favorite joke
of winery owners

🍇 Basics of Winemaking

What does it take to make wine? Many North Carolina farmers have been asking themselves this question as they search for an alternative to the state's traditional cash crop, tobacco.

The first requirement is patience. Larry Ehlers of Chateau Laurinda emphasizes, "It's a long-term thing. I think in the wine or grape-growing business, you have to think in terms of 10 years, rather than two or five years. . . . Most businesses, you think you should be turning a profit in two years. In this business, I think you would have to be considered crazy to think that you could turn a profit in two years. I don't see how you could."

A significant planting of vine stock needs to be ordered a year in advance, and then the vines usually require two to three years to produce grapes and five to 10 years to reach maturity. In general, if a winemaker who wants to grow his own grapes starts now, he would, if lucky, uncork his first vintage in three to four years. Consequently, as Lillian Kroustalis of Westbend Vineyards advises, "it's never too early to plant a vineyard. If you don't use the grapes, fine, but get them in the ground."

The second requirement is effort. Growing grapes, like most farming, is labor intensive. Dennis Wynne of Biltmore Estate Winery says, "Everybody thinks a job in the vineyards is so romantic. It's hard, hard work. It's hot in the summer and cold in the winter." Grapevines require constant attention, and they are susceptible to excessive cold, heat, dryness, and moisture and to dozens of diseases. In short, grapes are a fragile, temperamental crop.

The third requirement is money. Almost everyone in the wine industry emphasizes the expense of the overall process. For example, one oak barrel can cost $800. To those considering entering the business, Dr. Robert McRitchie of Surry Community College's viticulture program advises, "Keep your day job." He says, "I'm accused of being flip about this, but I'm serious. Cash flow is a problem."

For those willing to make the commitment and put in the hours and the years, there are immense rewards, although at times these are more emotional than financial. At some point, almost every winemaker describes the process in religious, spiritual, or artistic terms. Consider Lucie T. Morton, who in *Winegrowing in Eastern America* says, "Harvest brings a kind of death to grapes, and destruction as they pass through the crusher-stemmer. But there is no doubt about the afterlife of grapes—they are reborn into wine—and there is a direct correlation between their life on a vine and their reincarnation on the palate. Wine can be heavenly, hellish, or somewhere in between. It is the job of all winegrowers to place at least some wines in the company of angels."

In more practical terms, making wine has two main parts: the growing of the grapes and the processing of the grapes.

Shelton Vineyards

Growing the Grapes: Viticulture

Most winemakers insist that wine is made in the vineyard. Some estimate that roughly 90 percent of a wine's quality comes from the grapes and 10 percent from the processing. Consequently, although good grapes can make a bad wine, an excellent wine can never be made from poor grapes.

Winemakers also are fond of talking about the *terroir*, or the distinctive environment in which their grapes are raised. Steve Shepard of RayLen Vineyards explains the concept of *terroir* by saying, "Every area is different. The growing season, and the soils, and the topography, and the climate, and all that is different. It's even different 10 miles from here, where the amount of rainfall varies even when the temperatures are consistent." The *terroir* and the varietal contribute to the grapes' taste. The multitude of ways these elements can combine account for the diversity and complexity of wines.

Geography

Where vines are planted can determine the quality and quantity of grapes at harvest time. Certain varietals are suited to particular geographical areas. For example, Germany, which is known for its Rieslings, does not produce much red wine. The reason, according to wine expert Kevin Zraly, is that the country's northern latitude results in a growing season that is too short. Even though most German vineyards are on south-facing hills to try to capture as much sunlight as possible, it usually is insufficient to adequately ripen red-wine grapes. Because North Carolina geography ranges from coastal islands to Mount Mitchell, the highest point east of the Mississippi, most varietals can be grown somewhere in the state.

Soil

The soil provides the vines with the water and mineral nutrients they need. In doing so, it affects the grapes' taste. For example, Marian Baldy, a viticulture scholar, explains that rich and heavy soils promote grassy flavors in Sauvignon Blanc. If, however, wine-growers want to increase the fruity flavors of this varietal, they might plant the vines in less fertile, shallower soil.

Particularly in the Piedmont region, North Carolina soil can be clayey or heavy, which puts more stress on the vines. This is not necessarily negative. Many people insist that success comes only with struggle. In fact, high-quality grapes can be grown in sandy soil—Martin Vineyards is planted on a sand dune—or even rocky soil. Graves, a region in France near Bordeaux, is known for the gravel in which the vines are grown. The Teensy Winery has a vineyard in soil that is so rocky that holes cannot be dug manually. Regardless of the type of soil, the key is good drainage. Where water collects, rot can develop. For vines that have life spans measured in decades, this can be devastating.

Climate

Like most agricultural products, grapes need sunshine, fairly warm temperatures, consistent rainfall, and a long growing season to flourish. A vineyard's optimal season is a mild winter, a wet spring to promote growth, and then a fairly dry ripening season—one with

New growth at Rockhouse Vineyards

warm days and cool nights. This increases the grapes' sugars, which will turn into alcohol during fermentation.

The diversity of North Carolina geography has created a variety of climate conditions. As writer Bill Lee notes, some places in the Appalachians have a climate similar to southern Canada, while areas south of Wilmington can be considered subtropical. Wineries in the mountains experience a great deal of rain. As a result, thin-skinned varietals like Chardonnay and Riesling are difficult to grow, and crops must be sprayed every two weeks to ensure that the grapes don't succumb to black rot and other moisture-related problems. Dennis Wynne explains that Riesling grapes grow in such tight clusters that "the problem is, once they start getting ripe and they get rain, they explode. There is nowhere to grow because the cluster is so tight. They expand and pop, and here comes the bees, ants, rot, and everything. So then you have to pick them, and the sugar is too low for what the winemaker wants to make." In contrast, at wineries by the sea, such as Moonrise Bay Vineyard, the ocean breezes immediately dry any moisture, so growers don't have to spray and Chardonnay does well. Although coastal vineyards must deal with sea breezes that dry out the fields and create a need for irrigation, the stable climate provides a good environment for delicate white-wine grapes.

In general, North Carolina's humidity is greater than that in other wine-producing regions, which means there are more problems with disease. In certain areas of the state, dramatic temperature shifts also cause difficulties. This is because vines go into a dormant period after the first frost and acclimate as temperatures cool. If a sudden freeze occurs during this acclimation stage, it can damage the vines. A warm spring combined with a late frost can cause similar problems. Steve Shepard notes that on the East Coast, "April is a notoriously unpredictable month." Grapes, particularly European varietals, require a relatively short dormant cycle and are susceptible to budding out too early and becoming vulnerable to cold snaps. In the mountains, frosts can occur even in mid-May. "We've had years where basically we've lost everything," Dennis Wynne points out.

Grapes

Traditionally, the state has been known for its sweet wines made from muscadine grapes. These grapes flourish in part because their thick skins allow them to thrive in the Southern heat. They are also much more resistant to diseases than thin-skinned European varietals. Consequently, they are relatively easy to grow. However, beginning in the 1970s, European grapes such as Chardonnay, Merlot, and Cabernet Sauvignon were planted in significant numbers. By the 1990s, the acreage of these grapes surpassed that of muscadines for the first time. Because large-scale production of European varietals in North Carolina is relatively new, the wineries planting them are still determining which work best. In some cases, this takes years. Westbend planted Viognier in 1991, and the vines grew for eight years without significant grape production. The different varietals on nearby acres were producing well, and there were no frosts or obvious problems. Finally, after a change in the trellising system, the vines began producing enough fruit to make a vintage.

Trellising, the spacing of vines, pruning, and irrigation all play a part in the development of grapes. Proper pruning can protect grapes against disease and slow the growth of overly vigorous vines. A thinning of a vine's grape bunches can lead the remaining ones to produce more plentiful fruit. Agricultural techniques in the vineyard affect vines' production and can alter the grapes' sugar content. Thus, quite literally, a wine can be shaped on the vine.

One of the most important decisions made in the vineyard is choosing when to pick the grapes. Harvest too soon, and the grapes haven't reached their potential. Wait too long, and the quality begins to decline, rot can set in, or the sugar content can change. For many reasons, including financial considerations, using a combination of mechanical and manual pickers is common. However, because grapes are delicate, most vineyards would prefer to harvest entirely by hand if possible. Many small wineries rely on the volunteer help of relatives, friends, and colleagues.

Processing the Grapes: Vinification

When the harvest arrives at the winery, the winemaker analyzes the fruit and begins to decide how best to bring out its quality. Shepard insists, "You can basically look at the grapes as they're coming in and taste the grapes and know if you're going to have really good wine or not."

Changing grapes into wine is a five-step process of fermentation, clarification (which removes suspended solids—the lees—from the liquid), stabilization (which ensures that the bottled wine won't become hazy or deteriorate), aging, and bottling. Although every winery follows these steps, each one develops its own techniques, according to its philosophy. Chatham Hill Winery emphasizes a minimalist approach and tries to let Mother Nature do as much work as possible. Shelton Vineyards prides itself on a gravity-flow technique, which means it has less of a reliance than most wineries on mechanical pumps to move liquids.

The overall process for making red wine and white wine is fundamentally the same, but during each step, there are key differences.

Initially, grapes for red wines are destemmed, while white-wine grapes are left "whole berry." All grapes are pressed. Then, since the grape skins give red wine its color, they remain in the juice. For white wines, the skins must be removed.

The grape juice, which is now called "must," is pumped into holding tanks. There, the fermentation process begins, as yeasts convert sugars to alcohol. Although a few wineries use the grapes' natural wild yeast, most add a commercial cultured yeast to ensure consistency. Some wineries introduce sulphur dioxide to kill the wild yeast before adding the industrial product. Others do not, relying on cold temperatures to stun the wild strain and introducing the cultured yeast to "overrun" it.

In the tanks, red wines are kept at a higher temperature than whites, which makes them ferment more quickly. After 10 to 15 days, the red wines are pressed and then transferred into oak casks for aging. Storage in wood allows for a slow oxidation of the wine, which, according to Boyd Morrison of California's Alexander Valley Winery, means the tannins "slowly find each other like the links in a chain coming together," thus creating a smoother, rounder wine. White wines, which are kept at temperatures as low as 45 degrees, take much longer to fully ferment. A white wine is kept in the vat for six to eight weeks, after which it can be aged in either stainless-steel tanks or wooden barrels. Many wineries offer "barrel-fermented" white wines, which are fermented and aged directly in oak casks. This can give them a smoother, often buttery, flavor. But Morrison cautions that "white wines tend to be more delicate and can be overpowered by the oak."

After the wines are produced and aged, they can be bottled directly or blended. By law, to be labeled a varietal, a wine must have at least 75 percent of that particular grape. Thus, a Merlot can be one-fourth Cabernet Sauvignon and still be called a Merlot. Some special blends are given a new name. RayLen has developed a wine it calls Carolinius, which is a blend of four varietals. Martin Vineyards offers an "Atlantis Meritage."

As the winemaker continually monitors the fermentation and aging, he or she makes decisions to steer the wine in a certain direction. It's a constant process of fine-tuning. Shepard admits, "I sometimes wake up at 3 A.M with an idea to change the wine." For example, fermentation may bring out a grape's citrus flavors, and he may decide to accent this. Or he may strive for a taste of va-

Barrel room at Westbend Vineyards

nilla, which often comes from oak barrels. A Sauvignon Blanc may have a grassy taste that needs to be countered. As Shepard says, "The grape gives a wine its aroma. The winemaker gives it its bouquet." He estimates that a winemaker makes 600 to 700 decisions during the process, each one of which could have resulted in a different wine.

Since so many variables and so many small factors affect chemistry, no two wines are alike. Westbend, Hanover Park, and RayLen have all made Chardonnays from grapes from Silver Creek Vineyards, yet each of their wines is distinctive. Marek Wojciechowski of Chatham Hill Winery says, "That's why this business is so interesting. With the same grapes, you can make wines that can taste so different." Even the water used to clean the equipment and rinse the grapes can affect the outcome. If one winery uses city water and a neighboring winery uses well water, their wines will differ.

Once a wine begins aging, the winemaker has only one more major decision: He or she must monitor the maturation and decide when to bottle. White wines are usually ready more quickly than red wines. Some can be bottled as soon as six months after the harvest date. Many red wines can be aged in wood for more than a year before being bottled. Although all wines will age further once bottled, this does not always improve them. Whites should usually be drunk within three years, while some reds, such as Merlot or Cabernet Sauvignon, will benefit from longer storage.

In trying to realize the grapes' potential, a winemaker must have a good palate, the ability to identify problems, an understanding of basic chemistry, and a feeling for *terroir*. He or she should have another quality as well. In talking about the process, Steve Shepard repeatedly returns to one word: *creativity*. He believes a winemaker must have a style, a flair, a creative sense. A person trained in chemistry who has a sense of timing can make a good wine, but making a great wine requires the skills of an artist.

Wineries of Western North Carolina

Biltmore Estate Winery
Cerminaro Vineyard
Chateau Laurinda
Ritler Ridge Vineyards
Rockhouse Vineyards
The Teensy Winery
Waldensian Heritage Wines
Windy Gap Vineyards

Biltmore Estate Winery
USED WITH PERMISSION FROM THE BILTMORE COMPANY, ASHEVILLE, NORTH CAROLINA

$\mathcal{B}$iltmore Estate Winery

One North Pack Square
Asheville, N.C. 28801
Phone: 800-543-2961 or 828-274-6333
Website: www.biltmore.com
On-line ordering available
Hours: Monday-Saturday, 11 A.M.-7 P.M.; Sunday, noon-7 P.M.
    except for Thanksgiving and Christmas
Tasting-room fee: Access to the winery is limited to those who buy tickets to Biltmore Estate, which cost $36. Once inside the winery, tasting of estate wines is free. Tasting of premium wines is $2 for one sample and $5 for three. All prices subject to change.

Winemaker: Bernard DeLille
First vines planted: 1971
First year as bonded winery: 1977
First wine release: 1977

Directions: The winery is on the grounds of Biltmore Estate in Asheville. Take Interstate 40 to Exit 50A. Go north on U.S. 25 for two blocks to the estate entrance.

When George Washington Vanderbilt visited Asheville in 1888, he liked the area so much that he decided to build a home here. Its 250 rooms—including 33 bedrooms and 43 bathrooms—make Biltmore the largest private residence in America. Designed by Richard Morris Hunt, the French-style château required hundreds of builders and artisans. Construction lasted from 1890 to 1895. The estate's grounds, which originally covered 125,000 acres, were equally impressive. They included a timber farm, a dairy farm, and 250 acres of formal and natural gardens created by landscape architect Frederick Law Olmsted, the designer of New York's Central Park.

Since the estate was designed to be self-sufficient, George Vanderbilt's grandson, William Amherst Vanderbilt Cecil, decided in 1971 that vineyards would be a suitable addition. As an experiment, a few acres of vines, including French-American hybrids such as Marechal Foch, were planted. In 1977, when it became clear that grapes could be grown here, the estate increased its plantings, established a bonded winery, and hired Philippe Jourdain as a winemaking consultant. He later served as winemaker. In the following decade, the dairy barn, one of the estate's original buildings, was renovated to make a 90,000-square-foot state-of-the-art winery. This commitment of resources has paid off. In the last 25 years, Biltmore wines have won hundreds of awards in national and international competitions.

When Jourdain retired in 1995, Bernard DeLille became wine master. DeLille insists, however, that considering a single person responsible for a wine is a mistake. He points out that in France, people don't know the names of winemakers. Instead, they know the names of owners or estates. "What is good in winemaking is that it's not the work of one person, it's teamwork from the vineyards on," he says.

One crucial member of the "Biltmore team" is vineyard manager Dennis Wynne, who joined the estate after finishing his horticulture degree in 1981. Wynne has seen the vineyards go through a number of changes. When he arrived, there were 50 acres of vines. In the next few years, the estate not only doubled its plantings but built a 40-acre lake to irrigate them. At its largest, the vineyards encompassed 140 acres, but it became clear that some varietals, particularly thin-skinned white grapes, simply don't grow well in the Blue Ridge environment. Consequently, a process of contraction and regrouping took place. The vineyards once included 35 acres of Sauvignon Blanc but now have none. From 30 acres of

Riesling, the estate is down to four.

Thanks to his more than 20 years of experience, Wynne has become an expert on the problems of growing grapes in the area. Geese, deer, and other wildlife destroy a certain percentage of each crop, but the vineyards' biggest enemy is fungus. The area usually gets a great deal of rain. "If we get thunderstorms in the afternoons, the vines will stay wet all night, and then we'll have fog in the morning," Wynne explains. "Sometimes, they can be wet 24 hours." Consequently, although Biltmore tries to be as organic as possible, the weather makes the vines so susceptible to rot that regular spraying is crucial. Wynne insists, "We're trying to use everything as safely as we can. We've gotten sprays that are safer and safer." It's a matter of personal concern for him and his crew. After all, he points out, "we work here, and we want to be here 20 and 30 more years."

Wynne and DeLille work closely together and clearly respect one another. In particular, the vineyard manager appreciates the wine master's understanding of grapes. For example, according to Wynne, unlike some winemakers, DeLille recognizes the importance of picking a crop even when its sugar level may not be optimal. "If it starts rotting, he'll say, 'Let's pick it now, and I'll do something with it,' " Wynne explains. "He knows you can't make good wine out of bad grapes. It's like cooking at home; if you've got rot in there, it doesn't matter what you do with it, it's going to be bad."

DeLille insists that the number-one mistake a winemaker can make is "overestimating the quality of the grapes. Some years, you have to say, 'Oh, with that, I cannot make a good red wine, I'll have to do a blush.' " He believes a winemaker must be realistic. "You have a grape, and your role is to interpret the potential of the grape and try to do the best you can with it," he says. "Never try to do more than the grapes can do."

Although visitors to Biltmore Estate Winery aren't able to see its vineyards, which are located away from the estate, there is plenty to do. A self-guided visit includes a video presentation and a great deal of information about wine, the winery, and the estate. At various points on the route, windows offer views of the winery's working areas, such as the barrel room and the champagne room. After going through the enormous tasting-room, where guests can sample estate wines, the visit ends at a gift shop that sells wines, gourmet food, Biltmore souvenirs, and other products. One area of the shop is devoted to cooking displays by chefs from Biltmore's restaurants. If visitors are hungry, they can picnic at one of the covered tables outside or eat at the next-door bistro.

Biltmore Estate Wine Company has established three labels: George Washington Vanderbilt premium vintages, Biltmore Estate Château Reserve, and Biltmore Estate Wines. The winery has been expanded several times and now has a tank capacity of 250,000 gallons. Because it produces over 100,000 cases a year, it buys a large quantity of grapes in addition to using the harvests from its own vineyards. Although it has usually relied on California fruit, the winery has begun working more with regional growers as vinifera plantings in the Southeast have increased. In fact, DeLille believes that in North Carolina, "we have the soil to make some wines with great personality."

Because of the amount of time, energy, and investment grape growing takes, DeLille says that some of the state's new vineyards "will be good, and some won't be good. Some, we will have to tell them, 'Find something else to do.' " Overall, however, he is optimistic about the North Carolina wine industry. "The more wineries you have, the more you will have the power of the market," he points out. "When you're alone, it's difficult." As the industry develops, he hopes it will establish its own identity. He insists, "You have to forget about French wine. You have to forget about California wine." With North Carolina grapes, a winemaker should make wine that will be unique. To do this, DeLille says, "you must discover and find out what is working and what is not working. You experiment. As winemakers, we don't create, we interpret. That's the fun part."

Bernard DeLille
USED WITH PERMISSION FROM THE BILTMORE COMPANY, ASHEVILLE, NORTH CAROLINA

Biltmore Estate Winery Wine List

 ### Whites
Chardonnay Sur Lies, American Chardonnay, Chenin Blanc, American Riesling, Sauvignon Blanc

 ### Rosés
Zinfandel Blanc de Noir, Cabernet Sauvignon Blanc de Noir

 ### Reds
Cabernet Sauvignon, Cardinal's Crest, Merlot

 ### Sparkling
Biltmore Estate Methode Champenoise Blanc de Blanc Brut, Biltmore Estate Methode Champenoise Blanc de Blanc Sec

Biltmore Estate Château Reserve

Château Reserve Chardonnay, Château Reserve Cabernet Sauvignon, Château Reserve Claret, Château Reserve Cabernet Franc, Château Reserve Methode Champenoise-Brut

Recipe Suggestion from Biltmore Estate Winery

Riesling Vinaigrette

2 cups Biltmore Estate American Riesling
½ cup honey
¼ cup white wine vinegar
1 teaspoon Dijon mustard
¼ cup balsamic vinegar
pinch of nutmeg

pinch of cinnamon
juice of 3 oranges
juice of 1 lime
¼ cup brown sugar
1 pint strawberries
5 cups oil

Combine all ingredients except oil and process in a blender or food processor. While processor is running, slowly incorporate oil. Adjust seasonings to taste.

Cerminaro Vineyard

4399 Wilkesboro Boulevard
Boomer, N.C. 28606
Phone: 828-754-9306
Fax: 828-757-3958
Website: www.cerminarovineyard.com
Hours: Saturday, noon-6 P.M., and by appointment
Tasting-room fee: none

Owners: Joe and Deborah Cerminaro
Winemaker: Joe Cerminaro
First vines planted: 1995
First year as bonded winery: 2001
First wine release: 2001

Directions: Take U.S. 421 to the N.C. 18 exit (Lenoir/ Taylorsville). Follow N.C. 18 north into Caldwell County. From the county line, go 2 miles. The winery is on the right on top of the hill.

To support his family, Joe Cerminaro spent 20 years in the navy and then 15 more as a mechanical engineer. But what he really wanted to be was a farmer. Having been raised in an Italian-American culture that valued wine, he "always had this dream of growing grapes." After moving with his wife, Deborah, to a 50-acre farm in the rolling hills of Caldwell County, he had his chance. Joe says, "I kept looking at the sun and the soil, and I thought, 'Grapes can grow here. I'm sure they can.' " In 1995, he planted vines on three-quarters of an acre as an experiment. They did so well that he and

Deborah began to consider growing more, both for fun and "as something to subsidize our retirement." After three years of research, they made the decision to establish a commercial vineyard and winery.

Although they are self-described "country people," the Cerminaros knew little about viticulture when they started. Deborah comes from a North Dakota farm, but her family grew wheat, a much different crop than grapes. Consequently, after reading books and talking to experts, the couple still had to learn about practical matters. Joe recalls their experience putting in holes for hundreds of posts. He drove a tractor with an auger while Deborah walked behind and indicated where he should drill by yelling, "Drop it. Drop it!" Joe says, "If anybody saw us, they must have thought, 'What a bunch of idiots.' " After a while, the auger no longer worked. Joe recalls, "I went to the farm implement place and asked, 'What's wrong with my auger? It quit drilling.' The man said, 'There's two teeth on the bottom to help you get started.' I said I didn't see those. They had worn out. We had worn out the drill bit and were trying to punch holes without it." Joe laughs. "It was funny."

In their conversation, the Cerminaros frequently use the word *fun*, even as they talk about the difficulties of the winery's first years. "We made some mistakes," Joe acknowledges, "but we've had a lot of good experiences, and we've had fun." After a moment, he admits, "About killed ourselves, though." Deborah agrees, saying that it was almost "a slow, happy death." She remembers one electrical storm when their new crusher/destemmer was outside but hadn't been grounded. She wanted to move it but was "shocked all to pieces" every time she came near. "Yeah," Joe laughs, "that was a learning experience."

Originally, the Cerminaros planted hybrids such as Leon Millot, because these tend to be hardy and able to survive frosts and cold snaps. "We're a small vineyard," Joe explains. "We can't afford to lose any grapes. If we lost three acres of grapes, we'd be wiped out." In recent years, however, they have begun to experiment with vinifera, including Cabernet Sauvignon, Merlot, Pinot Noir, Riesling,

Joe Cerminaro next to an old wine press

and Sangiovese. Although in the future these may result in the creation of some full-bodied wines, so far the winery has specialized in what Joe calls "fresh wines" or "early wines." He says, "We try to produce a soft wine with no heavy tannins." They want to produce "nice, easy-drinking wines" that appeal to "experimental wine drinkers" and even to people who believe they don't like red wines.

Like their wines, the Cerminaros are straightforward and unpretentious. If you go by the winery's booth at a festival, you might hear Joe tell someone, "Try this. If you don't like it, throw it in the trash over there. It's not for everyone." He acknowledges that he makes wines according to his tastes. For example, he planted the little-known varietal DeChaunac because he tried it and liked it. And even though people encourage him to grow Chambourcin, he just doesn't care for it. "There's a lot of different grapes out there," Joe points out. "You need to learn to enjoy the different kinds of wine. Ernest and Julio Gallo did a great job. They sold everybody on those few European wines, but there are so many other grapes out there that are good."

Cerminaro Vineyard

Cerminaro Vineyard produces between 400 and 700 cases a year. For the most part, Joe and Deborah do the work themselves. Joe admits being surprised at the effort required to crush their first harvest using a 125-year-old hand press. He remembers thinking, "Boy, this is a lot of work for a little bit of juice." Deborah points out, "Like any agricultural thing, it is a lot of work, but you feel so good about the final product. Maybe it wouldn't be quite as rewarding otherwise." The winery occasionally gets volunteers. When two Mormon missionaries came by and admitted that they wouldn't mind something to do, Joe said, "Come on out. You can help us put in posts and grapes." Each year, friends, neighbors, and even church groups help with the harvest. They pick in the morning, stopping before the grapes get too hot. Then Joe cooks a big Italian meal for lunch and puts out wines that were made the previous year. He says with satisfaction, "They have a good day. We have a good day."

Currently, the winery offers private tastings that include cheeses and olive oils. At some point, because Joe loves to cook, he and Deborah may consider hosting small dinners outside, where guests would have views of the vineyard, the woods, and the surrounding hills. The Cerminaros talk about future plans with caution, however. Joe's "hobby gone wild" has already taken over their basement, and they know that if they're not careful, it could take over their lives. Deborah speaks with pride about what they've accomplished. "You just only meet so many people who are so driven," she says of Joe. "That's how we know it's a passion, because he keeps going and going." She notes, however, that "because he is so passionate about it, you can end up doing nothing but that. You have to be careful to find a balance." Joe agrees. "There's more to life than wine," he says. If one of their 10 children becomes interested in the business, they might consider expanding. The winery could be moved from the basement to the barn, and additional acreage could be planted. But since the kids still, as Joe puts it, "think we're crazy," they intend to stay small.

Whatever the future holds, for now the Cerminaros enjoy having a vineyard in their backyard. Besides its beauty and the satisfaction of drinking their own wine with meals, there are other benefits. Deborah says, "Having fresh grapes to walk out and pick is so luxurious." As for Joe, he simply likes his life as a farmer: "It's a nice feeling when you get out there early in the morning and the sun's coming up. It's just a nice feeling."

Cerminaro Vineyard Wine List

 Whites
Cayuga White, Riesling, Seyval Blanc, Vidal Blanc, Vignoles

 Rosé
Cerminaro Vineyard Rosé

 Reds
Cabernet Sauvignon, Chancellor, DeChaunac, Leon Millot, Merlot, Sangiovese

Recommended Pairings from Cerminaro Vineyard

Seyval Blanc or Vignoles with chicken, fish, lobster, or grilled foods

Chancellor or DeChaunac with braised beef or Italian foods such as pasta and pizza

Chateau Laurinda

CHATEAU LAURINDA
1999 RIESLING

NORTH CAROLINA
Semi-Dry White Wine

ALCOHOL 12% BY VOLUME

690 Reeves Ridge Road
Sparta, N.C. 28675
Phone: 800-650-3236
Fax: 336-372-5529
Website: www.chateaulaurindawinery.com
Hours: Tuesday-Saturday, 10 A.M.-7 P.M.; Sunday, noon-5 P.M.
Tasting-room fee: none

Owners: Linda and Larry Ehlers
Winemaker: Larry Ehlers
First vines planted: 2001
First year as bonded winery: 1997
First wine release: 1997

Directions: From Interstate 77, take Exit 83 to U.S. 21 toward Sparta; from the Blue Ridge Parkway, take the U.S. 21 exit toward Sparta. Follow U.S. 21 through Sparta to U.S. 221 South. Turn right on N.C. 93. Go 1.5 miles to the second road on the left. The winery is on the right at the end of the paved road.

When Larry and Linda were young, they met, fell in love, and wanted to wed. Because they were underage, they needed the permission of their parents. Larry's father refused to give it, so, following the advice of Linda's father, the couple eloped. They drove across the New Jersey state line, headed south, and ended up getting married in North Carolina. It was a sign of things to come.

Years later, Larry and Linda Ehlers were making regular trips to North Carolina to buy special tires for cars that they raced as a

Linda and Larry Ehlers

hobby. The tire salesman kept urging them to move, saying, "You don't know what you're missing. This is God's country. You've got to get out of that rat race up there." Eventually, they decided he might be right. So they quit their jobs, sold their house, took their kids out of school, and formed "a caravan down the road." Now, almost 20 years later, they claim that they could never return to the stress that comes with living in the Northeast.

Larry and Linda first moved to China Grove, where they began renovating an old house. They became friends with a neighbor, Pete Faggart, a butcher who made muscadine wine from grapes on his property. Pete's hobby reignited an interest in Larry, who had grown up in a "European-style household" where wine was "considered a food." As a child, Larry had often helped his grandfather make German Riesling and fruit wines until, as he puts it, "I became more interested in girls than grapes." When Pete Faggart died in 1990, Larry was unwilling to let the grapes rot, so he arranged with Pete's family to take over the winemaking.

Larry became a "happy hobbyist," but his avocation sometimes caused problems. Linda remembers, "We had an old house, and the floor wasn't level, and [the juice] would kind of ferment all over the place while we were at work. I'd come home, and it would be running across the kitchen. I said, 'This has got to go.' "

Encouraged by enthusiastic responses to Larry's wine, they began to consider commercial winemaking. This time, it was Linda's father who advised them against it, insisting they were too old. "It's going to kill you," he said. Again undeterred, they founded Chateau Laurinda, a name that combines their first names.

Initially, they used Pete's old meat shop for the winery. Larry recalls, "That was happiness, having all these different coolers." Zoning issues, however, forced them to move. They relocated to Spencer. While Larry and Linda worked day jobs, their son, Steve, and his wife, Melissa, ran the winery's tasting room. Eventually, Larry and Linda began searching for land to establish a larger winery. They were intrigued when they heard about an old homestead in Alleghany County. Their realtor looked at the property and advised them against it, saying, "You don't want to come see this. It's in terrible shape. There's so much work that would have to be done." As usual, they resisted such conventional advice. Reminding the realtor about their talents as builders, Linda said, "Do me a favor. Go back to the house. Open your eyes and look at it for the potential that it could become." Soon, they received a call asking, "When are you coming?" In addition to the house, the property had room for a winery, land to grow grapes, and beautiful views of the countryside. They bought it immediately.

Built by some of the area's original settlers, the Reeves homestead dates to the late 1800s. Larry and Linda attempted to restore the building to its original state, as far as possible. They put in claw-foot tubs and pedestal sinks. They had the original oak floors sanded. They took down the wood paneling in a bedroom, planed the boards, and put them back up. While acknowledging that such work takes a great deal of time, Linda claims it's worth it. Now, she says, "the room is absolutely gorgeous." When the house is finished, Linda will be able to realize a longtime dream of running a bed-and-breakfast.

They compare their love of renovating buildings to their love of making wine. "You can feel the history of a house. It's like working with a grape," Larry says. "You think about the origins of it. In an old house, you can feel the tears and blood and the number of people who were born there." They have met many of the people who lived at the Reeves homestead. One woman in particular has been enthusiastic about their work. She has asked if she can be the bed-and-breakfast's first guest. They've agreed, but they have no intention of charging her. Their satisfaction will be that a Reeves family member will again sleep in the room where she was born 85 years ago.

People who stay at the bed-and-breakfast will have a variety of Chateau Laurinda wines to drink with their meals. Catering to different tastes, Larry and Linda make around 26 different types of wine, from Merlot to muscadine. These include 12 to 14 regular wines and 12 to 14 specialty ones, such as blueberry, raspberry, and plum. Because they make small batches throughout the year, the wine list continually changes.

Larry notes that when they started, there weren't many vinifera grapes available, but there were plenty of scuppernongs, cherries, berries, and other fruits. Consequently, "we sort of cut our eye-teeth in business on alternate fruits, or what are called alternate fruits, and we still specialize in those type of wines," he says. They use only North Carolina fruit. Larry speaks with enthusiasm about the state's crops: "We can go to different areas within an hour of here at different times of year and get superb fruit, which for a winemaker is almost a dream come true." He insists that many fruit wines—cherry, for example—have a complexity and richness that can rival those made from grapes. "We treat apple the same way we treat the best Merlot," he says. "We don't show partiality just because it is vinifera or American hybrid." Furthermore, he believes that fruit wines are more difficult to make. One reason is that most of the equipment on the market is designed for grapes. Another reason is that "grapes are a natural fermenter." According to Larry, "if you put grapes in a vat and don't do anything to them, just let them sit, they would make wine by themselves. Few fruits would do that."

Larry champions a diversity of wines. He is concerned that the state's growing industry will end up concentrating on only a few varietals and certain types of wine. "I know a lot of people look down on muscadine, the same as they do Concord, and it's somewhat sad to me," he says. "Some Indian made wine out of muscadine a thousand years before us white folks were here. You can't help but feel and sense that, when you work with a muscadine grape. . . . It offers you something totally different in wine than vinifera, but it is all-American."

According to Larry, "people who drink Chardonnay and Cabernet do the most writing and make the most noise," but they don't actually buy the most wine. Those who enjoy sweet

Chateau Laurinda wine bottles

and semisweet wines comprise the largest market segment, and they should not be ignored. Larry learned this the hard way. He ruefully remembers Chateau Laurinda's first show: "We went with 12 dry wines, and they wanted to show me the bus and send me back home." In those first years, Linda used to go to Château Morrisette in Virginia to buy cases of sweet wine for herself. "Boy," Larry says, "that hit home with me." Consequently, he began making sweet wines. "It's quite complex compared to making a dry wine," he says. "Making dry wine is a simple process. You can go to Florida on vacation and come back, and your wine will be ready. You cannot do a sweet wine like that." He was dubious of his early efforts, refusing to sell his blackberry wine. He thought it was "too earthy" and a "family wine." But Linda convinced him to take it to the Southern Christmas Show in Charlotte, and they sold every bottle. Today, the winery sells all it makes, a fact that Larry says Linda doesn't let him forget.

As a hobbyist, Larry developed a unique technique for monitoring wines. He would put some of each batch into a large glass jug, so he would be able to see the stages of fermentation. At first, he kept these carboys out of sight: "At our Spencer winery, I thought it was kind of seedy, so we generally didn't show people. It was a personal thing where I could tell what my wines were doing. It was like a worktable. Then the Salisbury Women's Club got loose in there one day, and they thought that we should 'make sure everyone sees this because it's so pretty.' So we do." In the new winery, Larry and Linda have a "glass room," where the row of jugs can be lit with a fluorescent light to show customers. The different colors and the varying amounts of sediment in each container fascinate visitors.

Chateau Laurinda's new winery opened in 2001. Designed and built by Larry and Linda, it encompasses 5,300 square feet and sits on a small hill. In addition to a large tasting room that includes a "hobbyist corner" with products for amateur winemakers, it has a conference room for meetings and a long porch with rocking chairs.

A tour of the winery will not reveal any large tanks, rows of oak barrels, or expensive machinery. Larry prefers to concentrate on 100-gallon batches fermented in steel. For years, the family—Larry, Linda, Steve, and Melissa—did everything manually. They even destemmed the grapes by hand, a six- to eight-hour task similar to plucking beans. Because he dislikes automation and was wary of unnecessary expenses, Larry debated for over a year about purchasing a mechanical destemmer. He even tried to convince everyone that the hours spent destemming amounted to quality time when they could talk. Finally, he bought a machine. When it did in 20 minutes a batch of grapes that would have taken the family eight hours, he "got some evil looks" from Linda and Melissa. He shakes his head at the memory. "They would have liked to get me a new mailing address."

Larry and Linda try to make their wines as organically as possible. They insist, for example, on "zero spraying" of the blackberries and plums they use. To have even more control of the final product, they intend eventually to grow some of their own grapes. They have begun testing various varietals on their land. They do not, however, plan on becoming too large. "We didn't go into it for wealth or size," Larry says. "There's lots of other businesses that you can make a lot more money a whole lot quicker. You have to do it for love of art, and that's why we do it. You want to produce a wine that is unique that reflects your personality and your area." Ultimately, Chateau Laurinda's goal is "to remain a true representative of this state, all different wines and not just grapes."

People said Larry and Linda's relationship wouldn't last. That was in 1965. In 2005, they will celebrate their 40th wedding anniversary. Most likely, they will have a party at Chateau Laurinda, another commitment people advised them against making. But the winery, like the relationship its name celebrates, promises to have a long, productive, happy life.

Chateau Laurinda Wine List

Chateau Laurinda produces wine year-round and often makes specialty wines in limited batches. Call or check the winery's website for availability.

 Whites
Chardonnay, Pinot Gris, Riesling, Scuppernong, Seyval Blanc

 Reds
Cabernet Franc, Cabernet Sauvignon, Chambourcin, Merlot, Muscadine, Pinot Noir, Syrah

 Fruit Wines
Apple, Blackberry, Cherry, Plum

Recipe Suggestions from Chateau Laurinda

Riesling Wine Cake

Cake

1 cup pecans, chopped fine	4 eggs
1 small box instant vanilla pudding	¼ cup oil
1 box butter recipe yellow cake mix	1 cup Chateau Laurinda Riesling Wine

Glaze

¼ pound (1 stick) butter	1 cup Chateau Laurinda Riesling Wine
1 cup sugar	

Additional Soaking

½ cup Chateau Laurinda Riesling Wine

Preheat oven to 350 degrees. Butter and flour a Bundt pan. Evenly sprinkle ½ cup pecans in bottom of pan. Add pudding mix, cake mix, eggs, oil, and 1 cup wine to a large mixing bowl. With an electric mixer on medium speed, blend for 2 minutes. Pour half the batter into prepared pan. Evenly sprinkle with remaining nuts and pour in remaining batter. Bake for 45 minutes.

Make glaze by combining butter, sugar, and 1 cup wine in a small saucepan. Cook over low heat, stirring occasionally, until butter and sugar are completely melted.

Cake is done when a toothpick inserted in middle comes out clean. Remove cake from oven and immediately pour glaze over cake. Allow cake to rest about 30 minutes until glaze is completely soaked in and cake is cooled. Invert pan on to cake plate to remove. Immediately pour remaining ½ cup wine over cake and cover with airtight lid. Don't worry if cake sweats. Allow cake to cool completely. Serve with Custard Sauce (see below). Makes 1 large cake.

Custard Sauce

This old-fashioned sauce is rich and delicious served over Riesling Wine Cake. It also can be frozen and served as rich, premium ice cream.

5 egg yolks	pinch of salt
⅔ cup sugar	dash of freshly ground nutmeg
2 cups heavy cream	3 tablespoons Chateau Laurinda
1 cup skim milk	Riesling Wine or Scuppernong Wine

Add a few cups of water to the bottom of a double boiler and heat over medium flame. In top of double boiler, whisk together egg yolks, sugar, cream, milk, salt, and nutmeg until well blended. Fit the double boiler together and continue to heat, stirring constantly with a wooden spoon. Bring mixture to between 165 and 180 degrees for 10 minutes, using a candy thermometer to check temperature. When done, mixture should leave a heavy coating on back of spoon. Stir in wine, then chill mixture until ready to serve. Makes about 4 cups.

Blackberry Wine Cake

Cake

1 box yellow cake mix	4 eggs
½ cup oil	1 cup Chateau Laurinda Blackberry Wine
1 box blackberry Jell-O or sparkling wild berry Jell-O	¾ cup nuts, chopped

Topping

¾ cup powdered sugar	½ cup Chateau Laurinda Blackberry Wine

Spray a Bundt or tube pan with Pam. Combine all ingredients except nuts. Sprinkle nuts in bottom of pan. Pour batter on top. Bake at 350 degrees for 45 to 50 minutes.

While cake is hot, combine powdered sugar and wine. Poke holes in cake and drizzle topping over cake while still in pan. Let stand for 1 hour before inverting on to cake plate.

Profile: Larry and Sue Kehoe, Owners, Silver Creek Vineyards

Until the late 1840s, most of the gold in the United States came from North Carolina, especially Burke County. Even today, Larry Kehoe occasionally finds people panning for it in the streams that cross his property. He, however, has discovered a different kind of gold, one that's not in the ground, but in grapes. In the last decade, his Silver Creek Vineyards has established a reputation for high-quality vinifera. Wines made from these grapes have won numerous awards.

Kehoe's involvement in wine began in 1966, when he went to Europe for the first time: "I found out that a glass of wine was 25 cents and a Coke was two or three dollars if you could get it, and I decided that I had to change my lifestyle." When he returned to the States, he joined the American Wine Society, planted an acre of vines as a hobby, and even became a stockholder in Tabor Hill Vineyards, Michigan's first premium winery (an investment that would later become worthless when the company went through bankruptcy). Over the years, while he worked as a research chemist, he pursued his interest in wine.

When Kehoe retired to North Carolina in 1992, he decided to see if his 57-acre farm would be good for grapes. Because it has an elevation between 1,400 and 1,500 feet, sloped hillsides facing east, and constant breezes, he thought it might be "a great site." Against the advice of agricultural experts, he initially planted six rows. "Those vines did so incredibly well that I just knew that there had to be something going on here," he says. Later, when he discovered Westbend Vineyards and learned "they had been there for 10 years at least at that point, and they were doing a super job," he became even more convinced that vinifera could be grown in the state. Since then, he has

Larry Kehoe

been instrumental in developing the state's industry. He helped found the North Carolina Winegrower's Association and has served for years as a board member of the North Carolina Grape Council.

For a while, Kehoe and his wife, Sue, also ran The Hickory Wine Shoppe. Larry says, "We had the best of all worlds . . . because we grew the grapes, and we sold our own wine in the wine shop." At one time, he even considered starting his own winery. In fact, he designed the basement of his house to meet federal regulations for bonded wineries. He realized, however, that as a winemaker, he had limitations. He says, "My problem is, as a chemist, my initial approach was to do all this chemistry on it. Then I went through this period when I was going to just let the grapes do what the grapes would do. Well, there's some sort of a medium in there. You've got to do some minimum chemistry, and you've got to grow good grapes."

Now, Kehoe devotes himself entirely to his vineyards. He notes with satisfaction that "each year, the grapes are getting better and better." In fact, Larry Ehlers of Chateau Laurinda calls him "the best grower in the state." Although few farmers in the area have followed his example thus far, Kehoe believes they will in the future. In particular, he says that the east-facing slopes along the foothills of the Brushy Mountains "would be excellent sites, and I'm sure that people will slowly discover them." Each year, he becomes even more convinced that the North Carolina wine industry has a bright future. He says, "My dream is that we can be one of the top five or 10 wine-producing states in the Union. This is just a neat place to grow grapes."

$\mathcal{R}$itler Ridge Vineyards

39 Little Piney Mountain Road
Candler, N.C. 28715
Phone: 828-280-0690
E-mail: jemtrr@ioa.com
Hours: Thursday-Saturday, 11 A.M.-5 P.M.; Sunday, noon-5 P.M.;
    and by appointment
Tasting-room fee: none

Owner: Tim Ritz
Winemaker: Tim Ritz
First vines planted: 1994
First year as bonded winery: 2000
First wine release: 2001

Directions: From Interstate 40, take Exit 44 for U.S. 19/23 South (which goes west). Turn right on U.S. 19 South and travel approximately 3.5 miles. Turn left on N.C. 151 South. Go approximately 3 miles to Piney Mountain Church Road. Turn right, drive approximately 0.5 mile, and turn on to Little Piney Mountain Road, a dirt road. The winery is up the hill at the end of the road.

Located on the side of Piney Mountain at an elevation of 2,600 feet, Ritler Ridge Vineyards can be found at the end of a gravel road tucked among red oak groves. The owner, Tim Ritz, likes the seclusion. Since he has spent much of his life as a social worker, a job that he still does part-time, working among the vines provides a soothing change from "dealing with life and death all the time." He finds viticulture satisfying because it usually involves a set of predictable results, "whereas when you're dealing with people, you're trying to help them grow or accept, but it's so unpredictable." However, Tim also recognizes similarities between his two professions. As a social worker who counsels people who are coping with illness and death, he tries to give them the support they need. As a vineyard owner, he tends the vines to get them through difficult times so that they bear fruit. Whether it's people or plants, Tim finds "beauty in growth."

One of the smallest wineries in the state, Ritler Ridge began when Tim and his wife bought land in Buncombe County in 1993. At first, he planned to grow just enough grapes to indulge a winemaking hobby. After four years, when his harvests had increased to where he could easily exceed his personal 200-gallon limit, he decided to pursue commercial winemaking. He planted more vines and built a winery the size of a garage next to his house.

High ridges and mountains surround the vineyards and protect them from certain diseases and from frost. Moisture, fog, and ice may gather in the valleys, but not among the vines. These benefits, however, come at a price. The vineyards, which are more than 100 feet higher than the winery, can be reached only by a steep, winding road. This makes them inaccessible to most heavy equipment. Once, Tim hired a backhoe operator to help clear the land, but after breaking a third hydraulic hose, the man said, "Don't bother to call me again. I won't come back." The following year, Tim offered him another job, and true to his word, the man refused it. Because a tractor cannot be used in the vineyards, Tim cultivates his four and a half acres completely by hand. The first two years, before he purchased an ATV to haul materials, he carried gallons of water and equipment to the vineyards on his back. By necessity, he grows his vinifera in a "French style," without an irrigation system. He waters the vines a lot in their first year, much less in their second, and then leaves them alone.

The vineyards' setting also means problems with wildlife. Yellow jackets wiped out one crop. "Ferocious" rabbits eat new plantings.

Quail and other birds feast on grapes. Tim remembers, "I came up here one morning and went down to the Shiraz, and the trellis lines went *brrrrrrrrrrrrroooooom!*" He had startled two coveys of quail feeding from the top and bottom wires. They ate so much Shiraz one year that he ended up with only two gallons, instead of an expected 15. Solutions are difficult to find, since bird netting usually is sold in rolls that have to be put on with a tractor. Other animals including groundhogs, turkeys, and foxes roam the vineyards as well. Tim believes he has even seen a cougar that supposedly lives in a nearby cave.

Although he appreciates the area's wildlife, Tim doesn't want to lose any grapes. Consequently, he strives for a balance in his agricultural practices as he tries to keep his vineyards as natural as possible and also productive. Having studied Buddhist meditation, Tim feels there is a "unity of things." He says, "I really feel that the world is one. When I'm with the grapes, trying to use as little insecticide as possible, trying to watch them so I don't have to use more fungicide than I need to, I'm trying to be as one with nature." After a moment of reflection, he laughs and adds, "As one as you can be when you take down a forest of red oak." He understands that pragmatic needs sometimes override a philosophical stance. He has looked into organic sprays, but he says the area simply gets too much rain: "People who try to go organic are somewhat successful in California. . . . I don't see how you could go organic in North Carolina." When he tried an organic copper spray, he didn't like the result. In fact, it killed many of his vines. According to Tim, "unfortunately, if you want a good product, you have to spray."

As in the vineyards, Tim does everything in the winery by hand, including bottling and labeling. It is an artisan's approach, which is not surprising, since, in between stints as a social worker, Tim supported himself as a weaver for 10 years. Currently, he makes between 400 and 700 gallons of wine a year. Because of the vineyards' small size and the vagaries of farming, he never knows exactly what vintages will be available or what blend he may create. At the moment, to make red wines, he grows Cabernet Franc, Cabernet

Tim Ritz

Sauvignon, and Shiraz. As for whites, he has decided to avoid Chardonnay because too many wineries make it badly. He says, "So much Chardonnay is over-oaked that I stopped drinking it." Instead, Ritler Ridge offers a Pinot Gris, which Tim believes is a more subtle wine with a range of flavors. He also feels a personal connection to the varietal, since both it and his grandfather come from Alsace. Eventually, he anticipates that the vineyards will expand to seven acres. In particular, he wants to explore growing more Riesling. He knows that it hasn't done well in North Carolina, but he hopes that by being small, he can "give it a little bit more attention and get more product."

In Ritler Ridge's tasting area, visitors can look over a short wall and see the four oak barrels and the small stainless-steel vats where Tim makes his wine. The area also contains items from Tim's career as an artist. There are pieces of his own work and that of others. For years, he has been collecting ceramic wine goblets, some of which are displayed on a shelf. A large still life of wine bottles and glasses painted by his mother hangs above the counter. She also did the paintings featured on the winery's labels.

When Tim's mother wants to visit her work or her son, she doesn't have to travel far, since she lives midway between the winery and the vineyards. Tim remembers when she first saw the area. She turned to him and said, "I bet that would be a nice spot for a round house." And, Tim says with a laugh, she just happened to know about a nearby company that manufactured round houses. Tim agreed to take her there so they could look at the designs. He explains, "Since she was a little girl, she wanted to live in a round house with windows." So they built her one. "She just loves it," Tim says. At some point, he plans to relocate the small tasting area to the large lower level of the round house.

Whether it's taking care of his family, his patients, or his vines, Tim does so not simply from a feeling of obligation, but because it brings him pleasure. "I'm a firm believer in doing what you enjoy," he says. He advises his sons, "If you go to work for two weeks in a row and you're unhappy every day for two weeks, get out. It's not worth it."

For now, running Ritler Ridge makes him happy. Although it takes an enormous amount of time, energy, and money, it is, Tim insists, "a labor of love."

Ritler Ridge Vineyards Wine List

Whites
Pinot Gris, Riesling (blend), White Table Wine

Reds
Cabernet Franc, Cabernet Sauvignon, Red Table Wine, Shiraz (blend)

Recommended Pairings from Ritler Ridge Vineyards

Tim keeps a copy of *New American Cuisine* in the tasting room. It contains several recipes that he feels go well with his wines. In particular, Ritler Ridge Pinot Gris goes well with salmon dishes, crab croquettes, and salsas.

*R*ockhouse Vineyards

1525 Turner Road
Tryon, N.C. 28782
Phone: 828-863-2784
Website: www.rockhousevineyards.com
On-line ordering available
E-mail: mail@rockhousevineyards.com
Hours: Thursday-Sunday, 1-5 P.M., or by appointment;
    closed January, February, and major holidays
Tasting-room fee: none

Owners: Lee Griffin and Marsha Cassedy
Winemaker: Lee Griffin
First vines planted: 1991
First year as bonded winery: 1998
First wine release: 1999

Directions: From U.S. 74, take Exit 167 (N.C. 9, Mill Spring/New Prospect). Travel south 2.2 miles to Turner Road, turn left, and drive 1.5 miles to the vineyard entrance. From Spartanburg/Greenville, South Carolina, take Interstate 26 West to Exit 1 (S.C. 14/Landrum Highway). Turn right and travel east for 6 miles to N.C. 9. Turn left, travel 1 mile to Turner Road, turn right, and drive 1.5 miles to the vineyard entrance.

At first, the stone farmhouse that gives Rockhouse Vineyards its name seems ordinary. As you look at its walls, however, you begin to notice much more. Embedded in the mortar is an amazing array of geologic specimens: huge chunks of quartz and silica, fossils and shells, odd bits of modern-day glass shards, and various found objects. Built over the course of 10 years, the house contains rocks from at least 14 states.

Attracted to the house's unique design and its beautiful location in the foothills of the Blue Ridge Mountains, Marsha Cassedy and Lee Griffin bought the property in 1989. Since they lived and worked in Charlotte, the farm provided a relaxing weekend retreat. Marsha remembers, "We would come and sit on the porch and read. Our daughter was young, and she would dig in the dirt, climb trees, and just play. It was wonderful." Then, in 1991, with their daughter and her cousins helping, the couple planted four dozen vines by hand with a posthole digger. Although for years they had toured vineyards all over the world and toyed with the idea of one day having their own, they "started off thinking we were just going to have enough grapes for a hobby," according to Lee. Marsha adds, "It was a lark at that point, and it mushroomed bit by bit. As soon as we got a crop, the whole 'weekend retreat' thing changed." They discovered they had a far larger harvest than they could realistically keep for themselves: "We looked at all those grapes and said, 'Oh, my God, what are we going to do? We might as well see if we can make wine that other people will want to drink.' " That was the beginning of Rockhouse Vineyards.

The success of the grapes wasn't altogether surprising, considering the area's history. There have been commercial vineyards in Tryon since the late 1800s, when the region was known for its table grapes, such as Niagaras and Delawares. During the summers, local farmers would take their crops to the train station and sell them to people traveling to the mountains to escape the Southern heat. For decades, the area also had a substantial peach and apple industry. Fruit grows well here because of a thermal belt that protects crops from extremes of heat and cold. The hills and the soil, a mixture of clay and loam, offer good drainage, while the 1,100-foot elevation ensures a combination of warm days and cool nights. In fact, according to Lee, a survey map charting the state's winegrowing areas has "a line along the foothills of the Blue Ridge Mountains showing

Lee Griffin checking the vines of Rockhouse Vineyards

where the best place for grapes would be." Rockhouse Vineyards is on that line.

Prior to buying the land, Lee and Marsha "hadn't grown a tomato." Consequently, in the winery's early years, they had to educate themselves about viticulture. They read, talked to people, and continued to tour vineyards, now with a professional interest, taking reams of notes and hundreds of slides. Before proceeding, however, they had to solve some key problems, such as a lack of water. Initially, the family couldn't even shower without the farmhouse's well running dry. Lee and Marsha hired a company to dig a new well. On the first try, the workers discovered "so much water, you couldn't even measure it," Marsha recalls. "It was unbelievable. That was a sign: 'Okay, we are supposed to do this because we now have water.' It really was amazing."

Each year as they planted more vines, Marsha says, "I kept looking at Lee and asking, 'What are we doing? What is the plan here?' " They didn't have one. The winery "just sort of evolved." Lee admits, "Initially, we did it the wrong way. We planted just a few vines of several varieties as an experiment to see what would grow. The problem with doing it that way is that you can't produce enough wine of any single variety to make it economically worthwhile." Although they found that almost every varietal would grow, they decided to concentrate on vinifera grapes. They dedicated the vineyards' 10 acres to Cabernet Sauvignon, Merlot, Chardonnay, Viognier, and Cabernet Franc. The choice was dictated in part by personal tastes. They say of their wine, "We make it the way we like it."

In Rockhouse's first decade, a key figure in its development was Javier Calderon, who helped establish several of the state's vineyards. When he began assisting Lee and Marsha in 1993, the vineyards grew dramatically. In their first year, Lee and Marsha had planted 48 vines in two days; with Javier, they planted 2,000 in a day. He taught them a great deal and became, according to Marsha, "so much a part of this place. A huge part." Tragically, he was killed in 2001. It's a loss that still affects Lee and Marsha on both a professional and a personal level. "Losing Javier was very sad, for a lot of reasons," Marsha says. "He was so trusted, so competent, and, above all, such a great friend."

Since opening Rockhouse to the public in the summer of 2001, the couple has relied on local retiree Jay Adams to run the tasting room. A noted beer maker with a Ph.D. in genetics, Adams provides a wealth of scientific expertise. He laughs that his wife, Arlene, volunteered him for the job. According to Adams, when she heard that Lee and Marsha needed help, she said, "Boy, do I have the guy for you." He enjoys the work and notes that the building's unique construction helps him: "When we're in the tasting room and people come in here who are younger, I tell them that there is a DeSoto horn button in the wall outside the barrel room. When they say, 'What's a DeSoto?' I ask them for their ID."

Thanks to the tourism signs on the highway and an increasing public awareness of North Carolina wineries, Lee and Marsha find themselves having to guard against becoming too commercialized. What many people value about the winery, Lee says, is "the small- ness of it, the intimacy." After all, the wood-paneled tasting room used to be a living room, and to get there, you must walk by a kitchen with mint 1940s appliances. Lee and Marsha want to retain

Marsha Cassedy and Lee Griffin of Rockhouse Vineyards

this personal quality. Their attitude shows in their marketing approach, which is understated, the majority of their time and effort being focused on winemaking.

Since they still live in Charlotte—where their "paying" jobs are—and commute to the vineyards, they don't have time for a lot of extras. Rockhouse doesn't sell shirts, hats, or wine-related items at the moment. According to Lee, the pressure they feel is "the pressure to make good wines." Their approach seems to work. Rockhouse's first releases in 1999 received enthusiastic responses. Soon, Rockhouse wines began winning medals. Lee and Marsha laugh that these awards were not only gratifying but also helped reassure their now-teenage daughter, Hadley. Skeptical about the merits of her parents' endeavors, she was less than thrilled to see a local newspaper article that featured a photograph of Lee and Marsha in bib overalls "looking like the *American Gothic* couple." Now, however, she appreciates what her parents have accomplished.

Though Rockhouse Vineyards is small, it rewards repeat visitors because there is always something new to contemplate. Guests enjoy the splendid views of rolling hills, old orchards, and the vineyards. In the tasting room, Lee, Marsha, and Jay Adams offer an easygoing hospitality that complements the tranquil location. Although Rockhouse doesn't sell food, people are encouraged to bring picnics and linger. Not long ago, a couple chose to celebrate their 50th wedding anniversary at the winery. They bought a bottle of Chardonnay, then spread a cloth on the porch table and took Spam sandwiches out of their picnic hamper. Jay remembers, "I went out and said, 'Spam sandwiches for your 50th anniversary?' And they said, 'That's all we could afford 50 years ago, so that's what we're celebrating with.' " Jay laughs, "Rockhouse wines go with everything. Even Spam."

Rockhouse Vineyards Wine List

Whites
Chardonnay, Viognier

Reds
Cabernet Franc, Cabernet Sauvignon, Merlot

Recipe Suggestion from Rockhouse Vineyards

White Bean Chili

This simple dish is great in the winter with any of Rockhouse's reds. It is equally tasty in the warmer months with a chilled Rockhouse Chardonnay.

1 medium onion, diced
½ green bell pepper, diced
2 4-ounce cans green chilies
1 tablespoon olive oil
2 pounds chicken breasts, diced
2 15-ounce cans white shoepeg corn
2 15-ounce cans Great Northern beans, divided
1 tablespoon garlic, minced
2 14-ounce cans chicken broth

¼ teaspoon white pepper
1 teaspoon salt
1 tablespoon parsley flakes
1 bay leaf
1 teaspoon cumin
1 teaspoon oregano
1 tablespoon jalapeño peppers, minced
dash of Tabasco

Sauté onions, peppers, and chilies in olive oil in a large stockpot until onions are tender. Add chicken and cook thoroughly, stirring often. Drain corn and beans. Purée half of beans. Add corn, whole beans, puréed beans, and remaining ingredients to pot. Simmer 30 minutes. Discard bay leaf. Makes 3 quarts plus 1½ cups. To freeze, cool well and transfer to freezer containers. (Note: This is a mild recipe. If you like your chili spicier, increase jalapeños and Tabasco to taste.)

Profile: Gary Simmers, Landwirt Bottling

The Simmerses

At first, the attention caught Gary Simmers off guard, but now, when he pulls his tractor-trailer next to a winery, he's not surprised to find a crowd. His mobile bottling line fascinates people. They like to watch as wine gets pumped from a barrel room to his truck and cases of labeled bottles emerge from the trailer and slide down its back ramp. Simmers remembers the first time he did a job in Kentucky: "The next day, that was in 32 newspapers. Thirty-two! I didn't realize the *Mayflower* had landed again."

His business solves a problem that many small and mid-sized wineries have. Bottling and labeling wine by hand takes an enormous amount of time, yet the average bottling line costs around $200,000. Many wineries find themselves unable to afford the time of the one method or the expense of the other. By using Landwirt Bottling, they get the benefits of an automated line without having to make a substantial capital investment.

Simmers knew there was a need for such a service because he owns a winery. When it was "faced with the bottling situation," he realized "what the cost implications were for the average winery" and decided to explore alternatives. Having heard about mobile bottling units in California, he examined how they worked. Then he designed his own. Completely self-contained and boasting its own power supply, his line can average 3,000 bottles an hour, or 50 bottles a minute. All he needs is a place to park the trailer, a water source, and a labor crew. Although he began the business in 2000, he already bottles for over 30 wineries in North Carolina, Virginia, Kentucky, and Pennsylvania. He says, "I could go almost anywhere in the country if I wanted. I get calls from everywhere."

A former dairy farmer, Simmers enjoys working in the wine industry. He laughs at the memory of how he got started. In the early 1980s, a man named Charles Byers, who had studied viticulture in Europe, asked Simmers if he could experiment with vinifera on his farm. "I told him no," Simmers remembers. "My first thought was 'I don't need some guy in my way all the time,' for something that probably wasn't going to amount to anything." Later, he reconsidered: "There was a piece of ground that was useless to me because it was nothing but gravel and rock. It would not grow corn, soybean, or any of the things that we wanted. I thought, 'Well, I'll put this guy up there. He can't get in my way there.'" Byers spent a year evaluating the site. Then, Simmers says, "he started planting, and they did well, and he kept on planting, and the next thing I know, I had 14 acres of vines back there on this hill." People who bought the grapes "would win all the medals at all these competitions," and the vineyard developed a reputation as having "the best grapes around." Eventually, the vineyard's success led to the establishment of a winery. Ironically, Simmers now has so much work at other wineries that he has had to scale back production at his own.

So far, Simmers has enjoyed his career as an itinerant bottler. He likes traveling, meeting people, and seeing their different approaches to winemaking. "I get a pleasure out of being able to provide them a service," he says. His involvement in the wine industry has meant the end of his dairy operations, but Simmers doesn't mind. He laughs, "At my age, it seems like I enjoy talking to people more than animals."

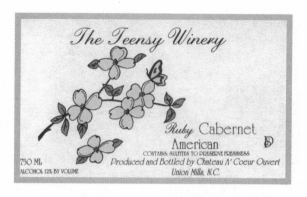

The Teensy Winery

3661 Painters Gap Road
Union Mills, N.C. 28167
Phone: 828-287-7763
Hours: By appointment

Owner: Bob Howard
Winemaker: Bob Howard
First vines planted: 1984
First year as bonded winery: 1986
First wine release: 1987

Directions: Take Interstate 40 to U.S. 221 South (the
Rutherfordton exit). Follow U.S. 221 South to Thermal City.
Turn right on Gilkey School Road. Take the left fork on to
Painters Gap Road and drive approximately 8 miles. The
winery is on the left.

Located in the basement of Bob Howard's house, the Teensy Winery is true to its name. Bob points out that he has the same equipment as a "normal" winery, only most of it is smaller. He says, "We're
the Mini-Me of wineries in North Carolina." When he gets a harvest from his vines, the winery produces around 300 gallons, and
whatever he makes "just doesn't stick around." He doesn't, how-

Bob Howard, owner of The Teensy Winery

ever, always have a harvest. For the past five years, black rot has infected the vines and prevented the grapes from ripening. After experimenting with different pruning and spraying programs, Bob believes he has finally "turned the corner" and figured out how to control the disease.

Bob's winemaking career started in Florida. A friend had an orange grove, so "just for the fun of it," they taught themselves how to make orange wine. He insists that it wasn't bad, sweet with a high alcohol content—"kind of like a Muscatel," Bob says. "You just didn't sit down and drink a lot of it. You drank a small amount and said, 'Yeah, that's pretty good.' " When he and his family moved to the mountains of North Carolina, he decided to plant a small vineyard and to try making European-style wines.

Bob laughs at the memory of getting his vines in the mail: "It's really depressing when you order these five-dollar vines, and they send you a box that's got nothing but a bunch of twigs and sticks. You think, 'My word, I've been had.' " After weeks of digging holes in the rocky soil and carefully planting 500 cuttings of Cabernet, Merlot, and Chardonnay, he went on a trip with his wife, only to realize "there's something wrong. These pants don't fit." He weighed himself and discovered he had lost 11 pounds putting in the vine-yard. The work paid off. The next year, the vines "exploded out of the ground, and the following year, it was all I could do to keep up with them. They literally were begging to grow here."

Bob's wife advised him, "If you're going to do this, really do it." So when he ordered his vines, he also got the government application to become a bonded winery. But he didn't fill it out right away. Then, "after two years walking around the table, I decided, 'Yeah, let's go ahead and do this for real.' When I sent the forms in [to the Bureau of Alcohol, Tobacco and Firearms], they were shocked. They said, 'These are obsolete forms. Where did you get these?' I said, 'I got them from you, where else?' " After receiving new forms, Bob started the process again. When the application was finally approved, he became the only legal maker of alcoholic beverages in Rutherford County.

To prepare himself for his first crush, Bob bought book after book. He insists that if you want to learn, "you just keep reading. Knowledge is power. Those are the three most important words in the world." He says that, as a winemaker, "a nice quality Cabernet is what I'm always shooting for," but really, "the goal is to have a good time." So far, he has been pleased with the results, which have received "good compliments from pretty intelligent wine people." He laughs that no one has ever complained except to say, "You mean you don't have any more?"

Although he does most of the work himself, Bob gets friends to help during harvests. He points out that most people "normally don't ever get a chance to do something like this, so it's a great enjoyment and fellowship when folks come out and get together." His friends have been surprised by the effort involved. They think it's going to be a lark, something like a Lucille Ball episode. Instead, they find themselves working hard and sweating heavily.

For Bob, the winery's small size makes it manageable. There is, he believes, an economy of scale. He and his wife own the equipment and operate with relatively low expenses. "If we don't make it, it doesn't hurt us at all," he says. "Some people are financed to the hilt, and they've got to produce. We're not in that position." If Teensy were to increase production to thousands of gallons, Bob would have to borrow money, and then "it becomes my master, instead of me being its master." And he has only a limited amount of time to invest in the work. In addition to owning Teensy, Bob is a commercial pilot, a flight instructor, an insurance agent, and the president of an Internet service provider. All of these jobs make him appreciate working in the vineyard because "it's a good chance to concentrate on something else besides the other multiple things I do. It's a time to contemplate."

Bob enjoys what he calls "a unique business," one that he feels is an art form. Even his battle with black rot hasn't dampened his enthusiasm. In fact, he has never considered quitting. For one, when he has a batch of wine fermenting downstairs, "the whole house smells so good, just so good, when it's cooking." Plus, "when you factor in the time and you factor in the taxes" and, most importantly, "when you factor in the joy," he figures that he always comes out ahead.

The Teensy Winery Wine List

White
Chardonnay

Reds
Cabernet Sauvignon, Merlot

$\mathcal{W}$aldensian Heritage Wines

4940 Villar Lane
Valdese, N.C. 28690
Phone: 828-879-3202
Website: www.allamericanwines.com/nc/waldensian/
    index.htm
E-mail: nc-waldensian@allamericanwineries.com
Hours: Thursday-Sunday, 1-6 P.M.; Monday-Wednesday,
    by appointment
Tasting-room fee: none

Owners: John Bounous, Carlton Caruso, Jr., Joel Dalmas,
    Debbie Garrou, Tom Garrou, Dr. Joe Jacumin,
    Freddy Leger, Brenda Leger, Dennis Powell
First year as bonded winery: 1989
First wine release: 1989

Directions: From Interstate 40, take Exit 112 and drive
north to Valdese. Go north on Eldred Street to North Laurel
Street. Follow North Laurel to Villar Lane. Turn left and
follow the signs to the winery.

Joel Dalmas

Waldensian Heritage Wines is a tinkerer's dream. Walk inside and you enter, as co-owner Joel Dalmas says, "a great big overgrown homemade operation." You won't see expanses of chrome, glass, and oak. Rather than being a showcase winery displaying what money can buy, Waldensian Heritage Wines is a tribute to what ingenuity and resourcefulness can fashion.

On tours, Joel gives the history of each piece of equipment. When the winery needed a filter, "we looked in a catalogue," he explains. "We found one that was exactly what we needed. Stainless steel. Made in Italy. Beautiful. Then we saw the price. Three thousand dollars! We closed that book up." Instead of buying a new one, the winemakers built the filter out of recycled equipment and odd parts, including an old typewriter stand, for a total cost of $106. Joel acknowledges that it may not look pretty, but it does the job. He remarks with pride, "The men involved in this winery are no youngsters. They've been around machinery all their lives." When they needed a bottle washer, they looked in the catalogue, only to see a $7,000 price. "We closed that book up!" Joel says again. They designed one using donated PVC piping. Although the winery's official motto is "Life is too short to drink bad wine," its unofficial slogan is "Plastic makes it possible."

Throughout the winery, needed items have been made from salvaged parts. Door handles consist of pipes and wires. Wine ferments in hundred-gallon vats that were purchased used from a textile plant for $10 apiece. When Joel has to acknowledge that some equipment, such as a labeler that can process 17 bottles a minute, had to be purchased new, the regret in his voice is obvious, and he quickly moves on. He would rather demonstrate a mechanism that shrinks foil around bottles' necks. The catalogue listed such a machine for $386. After closing the book, Joel figured out how the task could be done using a heat gun he bought at a flea market for $10.

Resourcefulness at the winery is a matter of practicality as well as a point of pride. The owners want to keep the wine as inexpensive as possible. They refuse to use oak barrels that cost between $500 and $800 each because, according to Joel, to do so would mean "we couldn't sell our wine for less than $20 a bottle." Instead, they age the wine in recycled plastic containers that a beverage company gives them for free. (In fact, the only place wooden barrels are used are as tables in the picnic area.) For labor, the winery relies entirely on volunteers and "Waldensian work parties," during which, Joel says with a smile, "we take Waldensian breaks, and we don't drink coffee." This cost-effectiveness guarantees the success of Waldensian Heritage Wines. Because profits are put back into the business, the owners don't get rich. Instead, they have the satisfaction of fulfilling part of the winery's mission, which, as its name implies, is to preserve Waldensian heritage.

The Waldensian Church dates to medieval times, when, to escape religious persecution, its followers moved to high valleys in the Cottian Alps of Europe. There, they developed a culture that combined their evangelical faith, their Italian heritage, and the French language. By the 1890s, population growth forced many to emigrate to America in search of land and better livelihoods. Moving from the western Piedmont of Italy to the western Piedmont of North Carolina, a group of Waldensians established the town of Valdese in 1893.

The community attracted immigrants for several decades. Joel Dalmas's parents, for example, came to the United States from Italy in the early 1900s. They married in New York City but didn't want to raise a family there because they felt the city was too enclosed, too dirty, and, as Joel puts it, "the sky isn't blue and the people have no manners." In 1913, they moved to the Valdese area and started a dairy farm. Born and raised on the farm, Joel has lived there his entire life except during World War II. He says of the war, "It took me four years to get back home." When he did, he found that "the cows were gone, but the buildings were still here."

Decades later, Joel and a group of Waldensian men converted one of those buildings—the 4,000-square-foot barn, built of stone and 30-foot timbers—into a winery. Pooling their resources, they formed the Villar Vintners of Valdese, a name that would later be changed to Waldensian Heritage Wines. They referred to themselves as the "Buonvino family" (the "Good Wine family"). Although the winery officially opened in 1989, everyone involved had been making wine for much longer. In fact, the owners claim over 250 years of collective experience and see themselves as part of a tradition that goes back centuries.

For generations, almost every Waldensian family made wine. From the time children were old enough to walk, they helped out. Joel still has a hundred-year-old grape-crushing tool that his father made from a dogwood limb, as well as a smaller version he was given to use as a child 70 years ago. He admits, however, that because making wine was a "secondary activity" for Waldensian families, much of what they produced wasn't very good. (When a reporter first quoted Joel as saying this, his neighbors called to warn him that "the old-timers will run you out of the country." He wasn't worried because "by that time, I was the old-timer.") By dedicating themselves to winemaking as a "primary endeavor," the winery's founders hoped to simultaneously preserve their tradition and improve the wines' quality.

The winemakers work mainly with Lambrusca-type grapes such as Concord and Niagara, which they buy from growers in New York's Finger Lakes region. They make both a traditional red and a traditional white wine, Heritage Burgundy Valdese and Blanc Royale, and they also offer successively sweeter versions of these. Joel admits that sweet wines are a concession to American, and especially Southern, tastes. At first, for the winemakers, "it went against the grain to make a sweet wine," but they discovered there existed a tremendous demand for it. Because the winemakers would like to buy North Carolina grapes, they have begun experimenting with local crops of Cabernet Franc and Cabernet Sauvignon. Using vinifera grapes, however, will mean the price of the wines will double, which makes the Waldensians uneasy. They want a quality inexpensive product.

The Waldensians' European heritage is evident not only in the wines but also at the winery itself, where the restroom doors say *Signiori* and *Signore* and where a boccia (Italian bowling) court runs the length of the building. A boccia tournament is held every June. Winners have their names engraved on a plaque displayed in the tasting room. Next to the court is a row of tables where people can picnic, sip a glass of wine, or simply enjoy the view of woods, a small planting of vines, and nearby hills.

Inside the winery's main room, photographs of the "Buonvino family" cover the walls. In one corner, a rack contains dozens of magazines about wine and winemaking. Another area displays wine-related items, from corkscrews to T-shirts. Because tables and chairs take up much of the space, the area feels like a community center, one permeated with the heavy, sweet smell that comes from making wine. Joel tells the story of a woman from the Charlotte German Club who was looking for a place to host a party. When she opened the winery's door, she took one step in, smelled the air, and said, "I'll take it." Others have been charmed by the space as well, booking it for birthdays, anniversaries, Christmas parties, and wedding receptions.

The popularity of Waldensian Heritage Wines means that after retiring from a 40-year career as an insurance agent, Joel now works more than ever. So many people visit on Saturdays and Sundays that sometimes he doesn't even get a chance to sit down. He doesn't mind, however. He is sharing a part of his heritage. And, as he insists, "making wine is a party." The winery's growth has also meant that the barn no longer provides enough space. Consequently, the owners have decided to expand to a nearby building. After they renovate its interior and build a deck around the exterior, they will be able to increase production from the current 5,000 gallons a year and will have room to host larger functions. Expansion, however, does not mean straying from the winery's frugal heritage. The "new" building was constructed in 1939 and has been used as a toolshed and workshop for years. It will be another example of Waldensian recycling.

Waldensian Heritage Wines

Waldensian Heritage Wines List

 ## Whites
Blanc Royal, Waldensian White Sweet

 ## Rosés
Blush Regal, Piedmont Rosé

 ## Reds
Heritage Burgundy Valdese, Burgundy Valdese, Villar Rouge Sweet

 ## Specialty wine
Millennium Deux (a blend of all Waldensian Heritage wines)

Recipe Suggestions from Waldensian Heritage Wines
(from Cooking with the Waldensians)

Shrimp Dip Supreme

2 8-ounce packages cream cheese, softened
½ cup mayonnaise
2 cloves garlic, pressed
2 teaspoons sugar
2 teaspoons prepared mustard

2 teaspoons onion, grated
1 pound shrimp, deveined
¼ cup parsley, chopped fine
6 tablespoons Waldensian White Wine

In a saucepan, stir cream cheese over low heat and blend in mayonnaise, garlic, sugar, mustard, and onions. Stir in shrimp and parsley. Add wine. Serve warm or cold with crackers.

Grilled Scampi with Prosciutto

1 cup Waldensian White Wine	freshly cracked peppercorns
1 cup virgin olive oil	24 scampi (large shrimp),
¼ cup fresh lemon juice	peeled and deveined
2 tablespoons Dijon mustard	24 whole large basil leaves
½ cup fresh basil, chopped	24 thin slices prosciutto, trimmed

Combine wine, oil, lemon juice, mustard, basil, and peppercorns and pour over shrimp in a bowl. Refrigerate 3 hours, turning shrimp occasionally. Remove shrimp from marinade, reserving marinade. Wrap middle of each shrimp first with a basil leaf and then a slice of prosciutto. Thread shrimp lengthwise on to metal skewers, starting at the head. Grill shrimp for several minutes on each side, basting with marinade.

Chicken Tiberio

2 pounds boneless chicken breasts	1 fresh tomato, chopped
breadcrumbs	pinch of sugar
6 tablespoons butter	¼ to ½ cup Waldensian Heritage
2 cloves garlic, minced	Burgundy Valdese
1 medium onion, chopped	1 teaspoon Italian herbs
3 tablespoons tomato paste	mozzarella cheese
8-ounce can tomato sauce	

Lightly grease a baking dish. Turn chicken lightly in breadcrumbs and set aside. In a large mixing bowl, combine butter, garlic, and onions. Cook in a microwave oven on full power for 3 to 4 minutes. Add tomato paste, tomato sauce, chopped tomatoes, sugar, wine to taste, and Italian herbs. Cook at full power for 5 minutes, stirring at least once. Arrange chicken in a baking dish and pour sauce over chicken. Top with mozzarella as desired. Cook at level 8 for 15 to 20 minutes.

$\mathcal{W}$indy Gap Vineyards

837 Pardue Farm Road
Ronda, N.C. 28670
Phone: 336-984-3926
Hours: Thursday and Friday, 2-6 P.M.; Saturday, 10 A.M.-6 P.M.;
    Sunday, 1-5 P.M.; and by appointment
Tasting-room fee: none

Owners: Allen and Sandra Hincher
Winemaker: Allen Hincher
First vines planted: 1996
First year as bonded winery: 2000
First wine release: 2002

Directions: From Interstate 77, take Exit 73B. Follow U.S. 421 North
for 6.5 miles to Exit 272 (Clingman Road). Drive approximately 0.5
mile on Clingman Road to Pardue Farm Road and turn left. Go 0.25
mile and turn left (again) on Pardue Farm Road. The winery is at
the end of the road.

Vacations seem simple. You travel to interesting places and meet
new people. Often, you take stock of your life, and, as you relax in
a romantic locale, you fantasize about making huge changes. These
daydreams appear harmless, but they can have unexpected conse-

quences. Just ask Allen and Sandra Hincher about how a vacation in Virginia dramatically altered their lives.

Enticed by the state's tourism promotions, the Hinchers drove through the Shenandoah Valley touring the area's wineries in the fall of 1995. They spent several days traveling country roads, tasting wine, and talking to owners and winemakers. The more they realized that the area resembled North Carolina's Wilkes County, where they were raised, the more an idea began to grow. For years, they had been working corporate jobs in Charlotte, and they were tired of the commutes, the days spent looking at computer screens, and the *Fortune* 500 mentality. They wanted to move back to the northern part of the state and wondered if a winery could provide a way to do that.

After their vacation, Allen and Sandra talked to family members who owned farmland near U.S. 421. At 1,100 feet in the foothills of the Brushy Mountains, it seemed a good place for grapes. According to Allen, "when we originally concocted the idea of planting vineyards on it, . . . [the family] all thought it was a fool's folly, but they said, 'If you want to plant it, go ahead and plant it.' " The Hinchers decided to start slowly. They put vines on one acre, thinking that if they didn't grow, they'd lose the price of a medium-sized new car. It was a calculated investment. A failure would be disappointing but not financially devastating. Thus, they sensibly began an endeavor that would end up putting an enormous strain on their energy, finances, and emotional resources.

Although they come from farming families, Allen and Sandra had never worked in the fields. They taught themselves as they went along. "We've learned it the hard way," Allen says. After renting a tractor, they had to figure out how to drive it. To find out how to care for vines, they pored over books, questioned people in the business, and went to seminars. The advice they received wasn't always the best. Following a friend's suggestion, they first planted the varietal Melody. "As it turned out, that was probably the worst varietal to plant in North Carolina because it's a French hybrid that's very, very vigorous," Allen admits. Melody requires twice as much time for pruning and being cared for as other varietals. Allen remembers, "It about killed us that first summer, trying to take care of that one acre." On Saturdays, they would drive 65 miles from their house on Lake Norman to the vineyards, work all day in the fields, and then drive home. On Sundays, they would make the 130-mile round-trip drive again, returning to the vineyards to put in another eight to 12 hours.

Allen notes, "We thought the first year was bad, but in the second year, '97, it was even worse because we had the trellis up. It was hell." The Hinchers refused to quit. Instead, they decided to expand. They planted four acres of Viognier, Cabernet Franc, Chardonel, and Chambourcin. Nothing, however, seemed to go smoothly. They bored 800 holes for new rootstock. The night before they intended to plant them, it rained 10 inches in 18 hours. Working in rain gear, the Hinchers and some loyal friends had to bail out the holes with milk jugs. Unfortunately, this proved one of the last rains in a summer of drought. Later, they had to bring in water trucks to ensure the young vines' survival. Each season brought new problems. Although a contractor had guaranteed a completion date of the building that would serve as both the winery and the Hinchers' new residence, it wasn't finished in time for the harvest. As a result, between five and six tons of grapes rotted on the vines because there was no place to put them. Allen says of those years, "My wife and I have a very strong relationship, to have made it through."

Luckily, the process of making wine has not been as difficult as growing grapes. For years, Allen was a serious hobbyist. He insists that there is no fundamental difference between making five gallons of wine and making 500. The key, he says, is to stay out of the way. According to Allen, if you grow good grapes and pick them at the right time, "the best thing the winemaker can do, other than dealing with problems that come up, is to intervene as little as possible." He concentrates on making small batches of no more than 500 gallons, so Windy Gap's wine list is subject to change. It usually includes three red wines, two whites (a Chardonnay and a

Sandra and Allen Hincher, Windy Gap Vineyards

Viognier, the flagship wine), and a sweet white blend of Chardonel and Melody called Three Dawg Nite, after the Hinchers' three basset hounds, Buddy, Rita, and Trouble.

After the winery was bonded in 2000, the Hinchers ran into additional difficulties. Following the terrorist attacks on September 11, 2001, the approval of wine labels became a low priority for the Bureau of Alcohol, Tobacco and Firearms. Consequently, Allen and Sandra had to delay releasing their first vintage and opening their tasting room. Finally, after years of struggle, Windy Gap Vineyards celebrated its grand opening in April 2002. At last, the Hinchers had the satisfaction of seeing people gather in a building they had designed, drinking wine they had made from grapes they had grown. Through persistence and determination, they had succeeded in fulfilling their vacation vision.

Although they hope the worst is behind them, Allen and Sandra know there will be more challenges ahead. Even so, they insist that the worst day in the field is better than the best day behind a computer terminal. They feel justifiably proud of what they have done. They wanted to change their lifestyle, and they have. They've moved back to the area where they grew up. They've established

Windy Gap Vineyards

their own business. Allen has quit his corporate job, trading in an hour-and-a-half commute for a 30-second one. Although the early years were difficult, "the payback," Allen says, gesturing around the tasting room overlooking the vineyards' seven acres, "is the joy of working here."

Windy Gap Vineyards Wine List

 ### Whites
Chardonnay, Three Dawg Nite (sweet), Viognier

 ### Reds
Cabernet Franc, Cabernet Sauvignon, Chambourcin, Rita's Red (sweet)

Recipe Suggestions from Windy Gap Vineyards

Sandra's Hot Crab Dip

1 tablespoon butter
½ cup blanched almonds, slivered
8 ounces cream cheese
3 tablespoons mayonnaise
2 tablespoons Windy Gap Viognier

½ teaspoon salt
1 teaspoon Worcestershire sauce
1 teaspoon Dijon mustard
8 ounces crabmeat, drained and flaked.

Melt butter in a saucepan and brown almonds. In a double boiler over hot (not boiling) water, combine cream cheese, mayonnaise, wine, salt, Worcestershire, and mustard. Cook until blended and heated through. Add crabmeat and half of the roasted almonds. Transfer to a chafing dish, sprinkle with remaining almonds, and keep warm. Serve with crackers or toast points and Windy Gap Viognier.

Al's Top-Secret BBQ Sauce for Baby Back Ribs or Chicken

Rub

2½ tablespoons
    coarsely ground black pepper
2½ tablespoons paprika
1½ tablespoons chili powder

1½ teaspoons celery salt
1¼ teaspoons garlic powder
¾ teaspoon dry mustard
⅛ teaspoon ground cinnamon

Combine all ingredients and sprinkle liberally on ribs or chicken. Sprinkle several more times during smoking. Near end of cooking, baste meat with Finishing Sauce.

Finishing Sauce

1 cup ketchup
¼ cup soy sauce
¼ cup cider vinegar
¼ cup apple juice
2 tablespoons Worcestershire sauce
¼ medium onion, grated fine

2 teaspoons green bell pepper, grated
¾ teaspoon garlic powder
¾ teaspoon ground white pepper
¼ to ½ cup molasses
¼ apple, peeled and grated

Combine all ingredients except apples in a medium saucepan. Simmer over low heat 5 to 10 minutes. Add apples and simmer 5 minutes more.

Use on ribs or chicken during last 5 minutes of grilling. Use excess as a table sauce. Serve with Windy Gap Cabernet Sauvignon or Chambourcin.

Profile: Stephen and Susan Lyons

Years ago, two teenage friends had an idea. Since they each had parents who were recently divorced, why not fix them up? Initially, Susan resisted her son's matchmaking efforts, but he persisted, saying, "Mom, it's just a day at Muir Beach for all of us. You love the beach." Finally, she agreed to spend time with Stephen. When he arrived at her house, Susan walked into the living room, where, she remembers, "I saw Stephen standing in profile looking at this painting by one of my favorite artists, Henry Richter. And he was looking at it with this expression on his face which is the way that I feel when I look at the painting. A sense of awe. And it was like, *Ta-dum! Aha! Ka-ching!*" The couple discovered they had many of the same tastes and life experiences. Susan laughs, "I think the boys probably got more than they bargained for because we fell in love, and then they had to share us with each other."

Among the tastes Stephen and Susan have in common are a love of wine and a sense of adventure, and these have led them to careers in the wine business. In fact, few people know as much about the state's industry as they do. A viticulture expert and a board member of the state's Grape Council, Stephen has directly installed or consulted on over 30 North Carolina vineyards and has worked with many

Susan and Stephen Lyons

of the wineries. Susan knows the wineries as well. As writer and publisher of the newsletter *On the Vine*, she regularly talks to owners and winemakers about the latest developments in the business.

Like many people, Stephen became involved in the field by chance. After earning a philosophy degree at Northeastern University, he supported himself as a landscaper, eventually becoming landscape manager at George Lucas's Skywalker Ranch in California. In the mid-1980s, Lucas decided to grow grapes because, Stephen explains, "Francis Coppola had just bought the old Inglenook mansion." When Stephen installed two acres for Lucas, he discovered that he enjoyed planting and tending vines. "It's kind of like having children, but they're growing a lot faster," he says. Eventually, after studying at Napa Valley College and working as the vineyard manager at Ravenswood, Stephen became a viticulture consultant. Part of his talent for planning new vineyards lies in his ability to examine a piece of land and understand its possibilities. If it's covered with trees, he can "see what's beyond the trees."

In 1996, the Lyonses decided to investigate opportunities outside California. They visited Asheville and liked the area so much that they decided to move to nearby Tryon. Stephen began working with several vineyards there, as well as on projects in the Yadkin Valley. Soon, the Lyonses realized they had arrived in North Carolina at a key time. Susan notes, "We're on the threshold of a new industry here. It's very exciting to be in on the ground floor."

After years of installing other people's vineyards, Stephen has begun to develop his own. In partnership with the Raffaldini family, he is helping to establish Raffaldini Vineyards. Located in Swan Creek Valley in the foothills of the Brushy Mountains, the winery will be an Italian-style villa. Its 50 acres of vineyards may include as many as 24 Italian varietals. Since many of these have never been grown on the East Coast, it will be another new adventure for Stephen.

Because the Lyonses know so much about the industry, they are often approached for information. When Susan realized that people's questions sometimes revealed "a real lack of communication, a real void," she decided to start *On the Vine*, which provides consumers and growers an overall picture of the state's wine grape industry. She enjoys producing the quarterly newsletter because, she says, "I love working with people. And I'm very curious." Publishing *On the Vine*, which she hopes will evolve into a monthly magazine, satisfies her curiosity by giving her an insider's knowledge of people in the industry. She says, "There're so many different personalities. What a cast of characters!" She believes, however, that they do have one thing in common: "They want to make their wines better wines. They're like artists. Blending wine is a highly creative process."

The Lyonses believe this is an exciting time to be growing grapes in the state, and they're proud of the industry's development. As Susan wrote in *On the Vine*'s first issue, "We want the world to know that North Carolina has seriously arrived as a producer of quality wine grapes and fine wines."

Wineries of Piedmont North Carolina

Chatham Hill Winery
Dennis Vineyards
Germanton Vineyard
and Winery
Hanover Park Vineyard
RagApple Lassie Vineyards
RayLen Vineyards
Shelton Vineyards
SilkHope Winery
Westbend Vineyards

*The tasting room of
Chatham Hill Winery*

Chatham Hill Winery

3500 Gateway Centre Boulevard, #200
Morrisville, N.C. 27560
Phone: 800-808-6768 or 919-380-7135
Fax: 919-380-1310
Website: www.chathamhillwine.com
On-line ordering available
E-mail: email@chathamhillwine.com
Hours: Wednesday-Saturday, 11 A.M.-6 P.M.; Sunday, 1-5 P.M.; or by
    appointment; extended summer hours include Tuesday,
    11 A.M.-5 P.M., from May to September
Tasting-room fee: Visitors may taste two non-reserve wines for free or
    pay $2 to sample all wines including reserves; groups of six or more
    may pay $4 per person to sample all wines and receive a Chatham
    Hill glass.

Owners: Marek Wojciechowski, Robert Henkens, and Paul Henkens
Winemaker: Marek Wojciechowski
First year as bonded winery: 1999
First wine release: 1999

Directions: From Interstate 40, take Exit 285 and proceed toward
Morrisville on Aviation Parkway. Take the first right, Gateway Centre
Boulevard. Go approximately 0.3 mile, then turn right on Northgate
Court at the sign for number 3500. The winery entrance is at the back of
the building.

Marek Wojciechowski

The conversation of Marek Wojciechowski, the winemaker at Chatham Hill Winery, contains two key words.

The first is *experiment*. Marek continually talks about experimenting with techniques, machinery, and processes. He believes in exploring possibilities. For example, the winery offers three types of Chardonnay: one that is unoaked and aged in stainless steel, one that is lightly oaked (either by being blended or spending less than six months in wooden barrels), and one that is fully oaked. This penchant for experimenting isn't surprising, considering Marek's background. A scientist with a Ph.D. in chemistry, he moved to North Carolina to become the research director at a biotechnology company. Consequently, he is one of only a few winemakers who feel equally comfortable talking about a grape's taste and its molecular structure. He approaches winemaking with a scientist's disciplined concentration, attention to detail, rigorous sanitation standards, and passion for discovery.

The second word Marek uses frequently is *classy*. In his experiments, he searches to create a wine with style, elegance, and class. Accomplishing this requires a mind that is not just scientific but artistic, too—particularly, Marek insists, when it comes to blending the wines. It also requires a commitment to high-quality materials. On tours, Marek points out with pride the stainless-steel equipment, the heavy bottles, the embossed Portuguese corks, and the distinctive labels—in short, all the elements needed to accomplish Chatham Hill's mission of producing premium fine wines.

The stylishness of the wines contrasts markedly with the winery itself. Visitors who expect the usual rural surroundings will be surprised. Chatham Hill Winery is located in a business park only two miles from Raleigh-Durham International Airport. A nondescript door leads into a small tasting room and sales area.

The location is the result of a key decision made by Marek and his partners, Robert Henkens and Steven Wegner (who has since left the business), during the winery's planning stages. Originally, they intended to buy land in Chatham County, whose geography and climate make it more suitable than surrounding counties for growing French varietals. They soon realized, however, that trying to simultaneously establish vineyards and a winery might overextend their resources. So they decided to concentrate on making wine rather than growing grapes and to spend money on production equipment instead of on an elaborate tasting room.

Although Chatham Hill doesn't grow the grapes, Marek works closely with the vineyards that do, particularly in the month before harvest. He carefully monitors the ripening process, tests the grapes, and tells the growers when to pick. The winery buys roughly 70 to 80 tons of grapes a year. Although it uses different sources, most of its grapes come from Black Wolf Vineyards, which Marek praises as "a showcase vineyard." In an exchange program, Chatham Hill takes all of the vineyards' crop and returns half of it in the form of wine bottled with Black Wolf labels.

As a winemaker, Marek likes "the heavy, full-bodied, more distinctive wines." He says, "In every wine, I try to emphasize fruitiness." His wines compare favorably with those of Europe and California. In fact, one winery employee, annoyed by a friend who kept insisting on the superiority of Italian wines, poured a Chatham Hill wine into an Italian bottle and gave it to him. Tasting it, the friend was ecstatic. "You see," he said, "if you want a good wine, you have to buy Italian." Although Marek likes this story, he points out that varietals grown here represent distinctive North Carolina versions. Even when wine is made in a particular style, the influence of geography—the *terroir*—leads Marek to tell people, "Don't expect it to taste like California because it will be different."

At first, Marek planned to focus on only a few wines, but he has since realized that a winery needs diverse offerings to appeal to different tastes. Making a narrow range of wines essentially tells people that the winemaker doesn't care what they want to drink, he feels. Although he was reluctant to make non-French wines, Marek began experimenting with French-American hybrids. He admits, "I'm glad that I did. These wines turned out very good. I can tailor more for the customer, and people appreciate it." He also has begun to make "picnic wines," which are semisweet. Regardless of the type of wine, he insists that "what we want Chatham Hill to mean to people is quality. If we make a sweet wine, we want it to be a good wine made from the best grapes."

Although Marek wants Chatham Hill to be synonymous with quality, he recognizes that it takes time to establish a brand name. He says that, even with a good product, "selling wine is difficult. It's as challenging as making it." In the first year, Marek personally marketed the wine. He remembers his first sale—10 cases to Wellspring in Raleigh. "I felt if I could sell 10 cases to every store, I'd be all set. Of course, it took a long while before I sold another 10 cases." Recognizing the need for a full-time sales staff, the winery hired Paul Henkens as director of sales and marketing. Under his direction, Chatham Hill developed an aggressive marketing plan that included the construction of an extensive website, participation in numerous festivals and community events, and collaborations with local restaurants. The winery also has established a club that offers member discounts, periodic shipments of special prerelease wines, and private tastings.

Club members and interested customers sometimes help bottle vintages. Local hobbyists help as well, exchanging labor for advice. Marek tests their wines, identifies problems, and offers suggestions. In fact, he plans to share his expertise more widely by helping to organize a winemakers' round table for the exchange of ideas. Marek believes in a community of shared information. It's a scientist's sensibility, a belief that the widespread distribution of ideas benefits everyone. He sees other wineries not as competitors, but as colleagues. It is also a practical position, since, as he says, "we're not judged by the state's best wine but by its worst."

Perhaps the advice Marek emphasizes the most, particularly to hobbyists, is the importance of reliable equipment. He learned this years ago in his native Poland when he attempted to make his first batch of wine. After crushing the grapes, he began fermenting them in a container in his apartment. Although he didn't realize it, the container was leaking. Gallons of liquid slowly dripped into a neighbor's downstairs apartment, staining the ceiling, the walls, and even the curtains purple. The neighbor was understandably furious, and it was years before Marek tried making wine again.

Marek gets no complaints from his current neighbors. The winery's business-park location has a number of advantages. Chatham Hill is the only winery in the Triangle area, and Marek has a 10-minute commute to his research job. But although the 3,000-square-foot space served the winery's initial needs, it is inadequate for future ones. Currently, Chatham Hill has a capacity of 4,000 to 5,000 cases. Marek would like to double that production in the near future, and eventually triple it to 15,000 cases a year. Although Chatham Hill plans to always keep a presence in Wake County, Marek and his partners would someday like to build a showcase winery where they could have larger gatherings, provide a picnic area, and host musical events. At some point, they may also establish vineyards in the Yadkin Valley. For now, however, the plan is to continue concentrating on making the best wine possible.

Chatham Hill Winery has enjoyed significant early success. Its wines have won numerous medals—in particular, the 1999 Cabernet Sauvignon earned an important gold in international competition. Perhaps an even more gratifying accolade for Marek, however, was one critic's description of the wine as "a *classy* Cabernet with a North Carolina twist."

Chatham Hill Winery Wine List

Whites
Chardonnay, Riesling, Sauvignon Blanc, Seyval Blanc, Viognier

Reds
Cabernet Sauvignon, Chambourcin, Merlot, Pinot Noir

Blends
Sweet Carolina Red, Sweet Carolina White, Christmas Wine

Recommended Pairings from Chatham Hill Winery

Chardonnay and grilled trout or chicken piccata

Riesling and hearty, rich cheeses, roasted Cornish hens, perch, or scallops

Sauvignon Blanc and rotisserie lemon-pepper chicken

Viognier and scallops, oysters, or fettuccine Alfredo

Cabernet Sauvignon and leg of lamb, filet mignon, or vegetable risotto

Chambourcin and seafood, pasta, or grilled pork

$\mathcal{D}$ennis Vineyards

24043 Endy Road
Albemarle, N.C. 28001
Phone: 800-230-1743 or 704-982-6090
Fax: 704-986-6128
Website: www.dennisvineyards.com
E-mail: mail@dennisvineyards.com
Hours: Monday-Saturday, 9 A.M.-6 P.M., and by appointment
Tasting-room fee: none

Owners: Pritchard and Sandon Dennis
Winemaker: Sandon Dennis
First vines planted: 1996
First year as bonded winery: 1997
First wine release: 1997

Directions: From U.S. 52, turn west on N.C. 24/27 toward
Charlotte. Go 5 miles to the Endy community and turn right on
Endy Road. The winery is on the left after 0.5 mile.

In 2001, *Sandon Dennis* and his father, Pritchard, had a difficult
decision to make. The family winery, Dennis Vineyards, had been
expanding rapidly and badly required additional space. The logical
solution seemed to be moving into a nearby house built in the 1940s
by Sandon's grandfather. It was a place, Sandon says, where "a
lot of families were started" and where several generations of
Dennises had lived. They discovered, however, that making the

building compliant with commercial codes would be tremendously expensive, and it still wouldn't provide enough space. Eventually, they had to accept the fact that they should tear the house down and construct a new building. It was a wrenching realization. Sandon's wife, Amy, left town the weekend of the demolition because she couldn't bear to watch.

Most major decisions at Dennis Vineyards involve both personal and business considerations because the winery is fundamentally a family venture. The land has been owned by Dennises for generations. The first wine was made in Pritchard's basement, and the original "tasting room" was his sunroom and back porch. Father and son work together in the vineyards and the winery. Amy keeps the books and manages the tasting room. Sandon and Amy's children occasionally run the label and bottling machines, and nieces and nephews help out as well. Even the winemaking recipe has a long family tradition. Pritchard's grandfather, the area's original mail carrier, was known for his homemade muscadine wine. Sandon laughs, "If anybody had the bellyache or they just wanted to get lit, they went to his house."

Pritchard inherited his grandfather's recipe and made wine as a hobbyist for years. He and his friends would pick grapes in the woods, and neighbors would bring him bucketfuls from vines on their property. He kept modifying and improving the recipe until the mid-1990s, when the wine was so good that Sandon became interested in making some himself. For a while, father and son engaged in a "battle of the batches." Then they started working together. Sandon remembers, "We were just going to have a glorified hobby. We were using the wine in church, in communion, and everybody fell in love with it and wanted to buy it." They began planting vines, but that "got out of hand, and it just kept snowballing." Eventually, they decided to go into commercial production. Now, Dennis Vineyards has over five acres of muscadine vines.

The Dennises regard muscadine grapes as part of the region's heritage, and the current rush by many people to grow vinifera puzzles them. Because muscadines are native plants, they grow well

Pritchard and Sandon Dennis of Dennis Vineyards

with little trouble, and they are less prone than vinifera to disease. Sandon explains, "They're really smart vines. They'll only hold the grapes that they can basically carry to maturity. If the load gets too heavy and they get stressed—for example, by a lack of water—they'll start dropping what they can't carry and ripen the rest up. They won't overload themselves. European grapes, you have to thin out." Muscadines make flavorful wines, and Sandon insists they improve with age. A five-year-old wine made from Carlos grapes will be "just as smooth as silk."

Although Sandon would like to hold some wine back and age it further, the winery doesn't have that luxury because it sells out almost every vintage. In its first five years, Dennis Vineyards went from making 500 gallons a year to 15,000, and the increased production still cannot keep up with demand. Much of the winery's success is due to the discovery of the health benefits of reservatrol, an antioxidant found in some red wines, particularly muscadine wines. According to Sandon, reservatrol has been proven to reduce cholesterol. It also may help with Parkinson's disease, Alzheimer's, certain types of cancers, and problems with blood pressure and the circulatory system. In 1998, researchers at Cornell University found that Dennis Vineyards' Noble wine contained the second-highest amount of reservatrol of all the wines it tested. This, Sandon says, "put us on the map." People began coming to the winery saying their doctors had sent them.

Many of Dennis Vineyards' customers swear by the wine's medicinal properties. One elderly lady claims that after she started drinking Dennis's Noble wine, her cholesterol dropped 60 points in six months and that her doctor told her, "Go back and get some more of that!" Another customer buys several cases at a time. His mother has Parkinson's disease, and he believes the wine helps her. She's not healing, but her mind stays sharper, and she doesn't have "the real bad days." He told Sandon, "If you start running low, let me know, and I'll come by and buy the year's supply." The Dennises themselves testify to the wine's benefits. Pritchard had a cholesterol count of over 300, and, according to Sandon, "he brought it down to 200 just by drinking the Noble wine alone. He didn't even change his diet." Even so, "sometimes he doesn't drink his wine like he ought to," Sandon says with mock concern. Sandon has brought his own high cholesterol down as well. Although doctors recommend three to four ounces of red wine a day, he admits with a laugh, "I push mine up to six or eight."

The Dennises are convinced that just being in the wine business provides health benefits. Sandon believes that the vineyards have prolonged his father's life. In 1985, Pritchard fell and tore an artery in his neck. At first, the doctors gave him three days to live, but after performing an operation that grafted a facial artery into his neck, they believed that he might live as long as 10 years. After a long and difficult recuperation, he followed medical advice and retired to the coast, where he fished and "started studying wine" in a serious way. Eight years later, his health had improved to the point that he moved back to Albemarle. A year after the doctors said he would be dead, Pritchard began the vineyards. Sandon says, "It's been unreal. I think if he hadn't come back and started this, I don't think he'd be here." Not only has Pritchard's health stayed strong, but his vision has improved. For years after the accident, he had problems with his sight and wore a patch over one eye. According to Sandon, "his vision straightened out" when he began working with the vines. Sandon says it can't be explained except by recognizing that "there are greater powers that be." Pritchard suggests that the Lord restored his sight to enable him to tend grapes. So almost every morning, that's what he does. He sets posts, irrigates the vines, and runs the tractor. Watching his father in the field, Sandon says, "He loves it out there."

Sandon loves the work as well. When researchers discovered the reservatrol amounts in Dennis Vineyards' grapes, they suggested, "You can make medicine, or you can make wine." He responded, "I'm here to make wine." Winemaking is his passion. Sometimes, he becomes so involved in the process that he works past midnight without realizing it. He puts in long hours willingly, an attitude he didn't have in his previous career. Before working full-time at the winery, he had a job in the computer industry, which "just burnt me totally out." Amy states bluntly, "He hated it." In contrast, Sandon says, winemaking "is probably one of the funnest things and the most rewarding things I've ever done." He insists that "no matter how bad the day was, I go home smiling. Not everyone can say that they've got a job they love. I love this. I can work day and night doing it."

Although he didn't like working in the industry, Sandon's computer background has been useful. For one, it enabled him to design the winery's labels, each of which displays a varietal or fruit. "What you see on the bottle is what's in the bottle," he says. The winery also offers special labels for Christmas and commemorative ones for events such as weddings and anniversaries. When the Cycle North Carolina tour went from Boone to Wilmington, it stopped at Dennis Vineyards. That afternoon, Sandon remembers, "there must have been $50,000 to $100,000 worth of bicycles scattered on the lawn." He designed a special label for the participants, then delivered their wine orders to them in Wilmington at the end of the tour. This kind of personal attention makes the winery a popular destination. Groups ranging from Porsche and Mustang car clubs to elementary-school teachers hold meetings at Dennis Vineyards.

It was to better accommodate them that the family built the new tasting room.

Although a bittersweet event, the construction of the new building has enabled the winery to grow. Sandon made sure that the tasting room included ties to the past. Not only does the new building have a shape similar to the former one, but the house's old kitchen was saved and installed next to the tasting room to allow catered events. It is a fitting symbol of the Dennises' effort to both pay tribute to their family history and address their present-day needs.

In the future, Sandon would like to put a pond and picnic tables in the nearby vineyards. He would also like to develop a you-pick orchard. In fact, he has many long-term projects, which isn't surprising, since he says, "I feel like I can be doing this until 60-plus and probably won't quit until I die. My dad won't, and his dad didn't." Sandon tells the story of his grandfather, who lived to be 91. At 78, he had open-heart surgery. Sandon says, laughing, "When he got out of surgery, he came to and said, 'I need to use the phone.' They said, 'Why?' He said, 'I've got to call my mother and tell her I'm okay.' They were like, 'You have a hot line to heaven?' He said, 'No, my mother's still alive.' She was 99 years old, and he had to call and reassure her." Sandon smiles, "I've got some long-lived people. My great-grandmother lived to 104, so I may be making wine for a long time."

Dennis Vineyards Wine List

All white and red wines come in dry, semisweet, and sweet versions.

 White
Carlos

Reds
Ison, Noble

Blends
Carnola (Carlos and Noble)

Fruit wines
Blueberry, Blackberry

Recipe Suggestion from Dennis Vineyards

Chicken and Mushroom Wine Sauce

4 boneless, skinless chicken breast halves	1 cup fresh mushrooms, sliced
4 tablespoons margarine	½ bottle Dennis Vineyards Carlos
10¾-ounce can cream of mushroom soup	(preferably dry)
(or cream of mushroom and garlic)	

Brown chicken breasts in margarine in a skillet. Add soup, mushrooms, and wine. Cover and simmer on low for about 30 minutes. Serve over rice.

Dennis Vineyards also recommends using its wines in stir-fry, spaghetti sauce, and crockpot dishes.

Profile: Michael Elsner, Executive Chef, The Wolf's Lair at Black Wolf Vineyards

Chef Michael Elsner
PHOTOGRAPH BY DWIGHT E. FLEGEL

Sometimes, Michael Elsner fears that, as a chef, he may be part of a dying breed. Unlike many restaurants that rely on a heat-and-serve method using canned and frozen ingredients, almost everything in Elsner's kitchen is made fresh from scratch. For example, in preparing many of his sauces, he first makes a stock using bones. This practice has served him well in a cooking career that has taken him all over the United States. It also has earned him acclaim. In addition to appearing on television programs such as *The Good Morning Show*, Elsner was voted one of the top 100 chefs in the country by the website chef2chef.net in 2002.

He began working in the industry at 13. He remembers, "There was a neighbor of ours who owned a restaurant, and his dishwasher called in sick, so he asked me if I could fill in. I said, 'Sure, why not?' And I learned that you get to eat for free in a restaurant when you work there." He worked in the restaurant through high school, learning the business, and then went to culinary school. Although he tried other careers, he says, "I guess I had salt and pepper in the veins, or whatever you say about somebody in this field."

As the executive chef at The Wolf's Lair, located at Black Wolf Vineyards, Elsner says that his job is "to recommend how to pair the wine with the food." In addition to creating lunch and dinner menus that go well with Black Wolf wines, he occasionally arranges special seven- to 11-course wine dinners. He likes to do

Black Wolf Vineyards Restaurant

these in the fall or winter, when "people can sit around the fireplace and get their socks knocked off." He says, "I'm very fortunate because we have some very, very nice wine." Although Chatham Hill Winery currently processes the vineyards' grapes, Black Wolf plans on opening its own winery in the future.

Elsner explains that, in pairing food and wine, "I get my inspiration from actually drinking the wine." As he tastes the wine alongside a loaf of good bread, fruits, and cheeses, he goes through a questioning process, asking, "What can I do with this bread? What can I do with this fruit? What can I do with this cheese?" This requires concentration. Elsner says, "You can't drink the wine and watch television." A person has to pay attention to a wine's "undertones" and ask, "What is that I taste? Is that butterscotch? Is that plum?" If, for example, it is plum, Elsner suggests that a plum sauce in a Chinese- or Mandarin-style dish would be a good pairing.

Elsner reads a great deal to help him learn of possible variations. For example, he points out that "Italians love strawberries with balsamic vinegar on it. Well, I expanded to balsamic syrup, which we were doing on portabellos at one time. Then you say, 'What would be better than that? Maybe I'll macerate the strawberries in a red wine or brandy.' " It's this constant process of experimenting with possibilities that Elsner enjoys.

He urges people to be more adventurous with food. Dining at a good restaurant should be an opportunity to experience new tastes. Consequently, instead of automatically insisting on tartar sauce with a fish dish or A-1 with a steak, people should "trust the chef and trust the wait staff" and try the sauce that has been prepared. For Elsner, eating well means being open to possibilities and appreciating food that has been carefully prepared. It doesn't, however, mean being pretentious. He insists, "To me, fine dining doesn't have to have a white tablecloth. I'd just as soon not have that. Fine dining is dining fine. You're eating good food."

Germanton Vineyard and Winery

3530 N.C. 8 and N.C. 65
Germanton, N.C. 27019
Phone: 800-322-2894 or 336-969-2075
Fax: 336-969-6559
Website: www.germantongallery.com
On-line ordering available
E-mail: sales@germantongallery.com
Hours: Tuesday-Friday, 10 A.M.-6 P.M.; Saturday, 9 A.M.-5 P.M.; call for
    Sunday hours
Tasting-room fee: none

Owners: David and Judy Simpson
First vines planted: early 1970s
First year as bonded winery: 1981
First wine release: 1981

Directions: From U.S. 52, take the N.C. 8 (Germanton Road) exit and go 7
miles north to Germanton. The winery and Germanton Gallery are on the
corner of N.C. 8 and Friendship Road.

One year, artist Jim Wilson was in Alaska's Denali National Park
taking a workshop with Robert Bateman, a world-famous artist and
environmentalist. After dinner one night, the discussion turned to
exhibitions. Someone asked Bateman what his most memorable show

was. He thought for a minute, then said, "There's this little gallery and winery in North Carolina that everybody ought to go to."

Not surprisingly, Wilson's friends David and Judy Simpson were pleased when they heard this story. They own the Germanton Gallery and the Germanton Vineyard and Winery, two businesses combined in one building. It's an arrangement the Simpsons feel "works great" because "people that enjoy good wine enjoy nice art, too." They have exhibited work by Bateman and other internationally known artists in their unpretentious space, a renovated gas station. David says, "When you walk through the front door of this little building, I think it's just a warm little place that kind of grabs you."

The history of the winery could be, Judy says, "a book in itself." It began as a type of cooperative in the 1970s. Several people who wanted to grow grapes started the winery on the farm of William "Big Bill" McGee. They also set up an experimental vineyard on his land in which they grew 18 different varietals. David remembers the day in 1981 when the winery opened for business: "We got up that morning, and there were people everywhere on the farm. People sleeping in sheds and in barns. They'd been there all night. There were people here from Kentucky, all over the country, to buy those first bottles of wine. . . . By midday, we realized that we were going to have to start limiting wine—so many bottles per person—so it would last. We sold out completely the first day."

Although many people were involved, Bill McGee was the

William "Big Bill" McGee
PHOTOGRAPH BY DAVID SIMPSON

winery's driving force. He served as president, accountant, salesman, and public-relations person. In short, according to David, "he took care of everything." Tragically, he was killed in 1986. "The farm was such a sad, sad place when he was gone," Judy remembers. "We just really had to start over then, and we, in most instances, have learned the hard way." Because they lived on the property, David and Judy were asked to take care of the winery. Finally, they decided to become partners in it as well. Eventually, they bought the others out.

As the Simpsons educated themselves about the wine business, they often went against conventional wisdom. For example, David notes that "in the beginning, a lot of people told us, 'Don't do blends' and 'Don't do sweet wines,' because people won't buy them. Well, every wine magazine that you pick up now, all they're talking about is blends." They encountered numerous problems, particularly with distributors. Judy says, "We've had everything go wrong and made every kind of mistake that you can think of." Nevertheless, they persisted, in part because they felt a responsibility to Bill McGee, whose photograph they keep above the tasting-room bar. Judy says, "He's why we keep doing it." David adds, "I hate that Bill can't be here to see all this [excitement about the Yadkin Valley] because his vision was wineries all over this area. Just like Napa Valley. He was so far ahead of his time in his dreams and beliefs."

The other half of the business, the Germanton Gallery, started with two dollars. One day while working at the R. J. Reynolds Tobacco Company, David was "sitting behind a cigarette machine and pretty much [thinking] that was where I was going to be the rest of my life." He bought a raffle ticket for two dollars and won. The prize was a Harley-Davidson motorcycle. Because he was interested in photography, he sold the Harley and used the money to buy framing equipment. This was the beginning of a gallery he ran out of his basement and where, as a matter of convenience, he began selling Germanton wine as well.

In the early years, the gallery concentrated on framing prints. Eventually, the focus changed to original works. By 1999, according to David, the Germanton Gallery was voted one of the top hundred galleries in the world. Several times, its annual miniature show, which focuses on small-scale works and takes place the first weekend in December, has been voted one of the best art shows in the country by *U.S. Art* magazine. The gallery attracts visitors from all over the world, a fact David attributes in part to its website, which gets more than 60,000 hits a month.

So many artists want to exhibit their work at the Germanton Gallery that the Simpsons must turn away hundreds of submissions each year. Judy believes the gallery appeals to artists for a simple reason: honesty. She says, "Artists are battered all over the world. Their art is taken for granted. They're mistreated." In contrast, the Simpsons treat them with respect. "We don't cheat them," David says. "So many gallery owners have the mind-set that if it wasn't for them, the artists wouldn't be there. We have the opposite mind-set. If it wasn't for the artists, we wouldn't be here."

After years of running the gallery out of a basement, the Simpsons saw an opportunity to expand when a nearby gas station went up for sale. Built in 1929, it had been abandoned for a long time. David remembers, "It looked so bad that I was the only one who showed up at the auction." After buying it, they renovated the space and filled it with art and other materials. David laughs, "We collect junk. Most everything in this building is stuff that we had stored in our sheds at the farm." In one corner, they put an oak bar top to serve as the winery's tasting "room"—or, as Judy calls it, "our liquid art department." Getting approval for the new facility, how-ever, was not easy. Although the combination of gallery and win-ery seemed natural to them, it caused problems for the state's regu-latory system. The various agencies didn't know how to classify the business. It took months to sort out the paperwork.

A display of Germanton wines fits nicely into a gallery envi-ronment because, as might be expected, the labels reflect the Simpsons' interest in art. The Germanton Vineyard and Winery does 10-color labels, which David believes is unique in the industry. Each wine features a different watercolor scene. The winery also does a variety of special labels and promotions. For example, one featured NASCAR legend Junior Johnson, who came to the gallery for a signing event. Others showcase artists. David points out, "An artist's dream is to get their work into a museum, but it's also now to get it on a wine label. It's really neat if you're doing a show or a charity or whatever to hand someone a bottle with your artwork on the label." The winery also does special labels to raise money for envi-ronmental groups, including the American Farmland Trust (the only nonprofit organization dedicated exclusively to preserving farmland) and the Florida Wildlife and Western Art Show.

The Simpsons feel a sense of responsibility and stewardship. They have worked hard to protect the legacy of Bill McGee. They believe strongly in preserving farmland and engaging in respon-sible practices that will protect it for the future. They regularly show-case environmental artists in the gallery. Every Memorial Day week-end, the gallery sponsors a show called "Things with Wings," in which the work, according to Judy, "has to have a pair of wings in the painting somewhere. It can be an airplane, a butterfly, a drag-onfly. It can be a statue in a park." As part of the exhibition, they bring to the gallery not only many of the artists, but also people from Wild Haven, Inc., an organization dedicated to nature educa-tion and wildlife rehabilitation, particularly of birds of prey.

Judy admits that the combination of winery and gallery "was nothing that we sought out to do. Some people ask how we had this wonderful vision. Well, we didn't have this wonderful vision. It just all happened." Now, however, they do have "a vision of the winery." They have begun making plans for a desperately needed expansion. Originally, the winery was scheduled to be housed in Bill McGee's old converted dairy barn for only five years. It has now been there for over 20. A few years ago, when their children returned to the farm and began having grandchildren, David and Judy stopped giving tours. Even so, "the kids have no privacy since they've moved back," Judy notes. "People knock on their doors at all hours wanting to buy wine. We even put a gate [posted], 'Keep out,' but people still pull up, open that gate, and go right on in." Consequently, David and Judy want to bring the various winery operations under one roof. They would like to build an energy-efficient space with a design that fits the environment so well it looks "like it's been there a hundred years."

David has a number of other long-range plans. He admits, "I'm a big dreamer." None of these plans, however, involves becoming a large, automated operation capable of producing tens of thousands of cases. He says, "We have no desire to be big. I'm glad Shelton, Westbend, and RayLen are doing what they're doing. It's good for everyone. But we want to stay small. We do everything literally by hand. We crush by hand. Press by hand. Bottle and label by hand. And that's the way we'd like to keep it." The Simpsons also want to preserve the business's intimate feel. Judy believes that "to feel good when you walk into a place, there has to be an ambiance in the place. Money won't do it. It's not a dollar amount. You walk into galleries, and even if they are big, fancy ones, if they don't feel good when you walk in there, you don't want to be there. The art doesn't look good to you. It doesn't feel good to you. That's what David and I bring to this. The love of what we're doing. The love to keep it going after all these years."

The winery requires a tremendous commitment. David says, "We work day and night. Seven days a week. My mom thinks I'm kidding her sometimes when I can't get over there all the time, but we leave the gallery and go to the winery and work at night and weekends." It's a tiring schedule, one the Simpsons insist they can maintain only because of the help of their son Michael McGee and their nephew Tommy Preston. Judy says, "Without them, we could not do this." Despite the work, the Simpsons don't regret what they regard as an adventure and "a great learning experience." David insists, "We're having fun. Life's too short not to." He believes in the value of what they're doing. He says with confidence, "The wine is good. The art's good. If you come here and experience this, you may not buy right away, but you'll be back."

Germanton Vineyard and Winery Wine List

 Whites
Chardonnay, Niagara, Seyval Blanc

 Rosé
Autumn Blush

 Reds
Sweet Red Wine, Chambourcin

Recommended Pairings from Germanton Vineyard and Winery

Chambourcin with steaks and pasta

Chardonnay, Autumn Blush, or Seyval Blanc with chicken or fish

Sweet Red or Niagara with after-dinner desserts

Hanover Park Vineyard

1927 Courtney-Huntsville Road
Yadkinville, N.C. 27055
Phone: 336-463-2875
Website: www.hanoverparkwines.com
E-mail: hanoverp@hanoverparkwines.com
Hours: Thursday and Friday, 4-6 P.M.; Saturday, noon-6 P.M.; and
     Sunday, 1-5 P.M.; call for extended summer hours
Tasting-room fee: none

Owners: Michael and Amy Helton
Winemaker: Michael Helton
First vines planted: 1997
First year as bonded winery: 1999
First wine release: 2000

Directions: From Interstate 40, take Exit 170, drive north for 9.8
miles on U.S. 601, and turn right on Courtney-Huntsville Road.
The vineyard is on the left after 1 mile. From U.S. 421, exit at U.S.
601 and go south for 4 miles. At the second blinking light, turn
on to Courtney-Huntsville Road. The vineyard is on the left after 1
mile.

You can walk around the entire grounds of Hanover Park Vineyard in minutes. Nevertheless, if you visit, be prepared to stay
awhile. The winery is located in a renovated farmhouse, and you
might want to relax on its porch or picnic next to the barn. Most

likely, you'll start talking with the owners, Michael and Amy Helton. Teachers, artists, and winemakers, they have created a comfortable space that encourages people to linger. Michael compares the winery to "the old general store with the potbellied stove," where "everyone passes through." He sees spending time with customers as the equivalent of a neighborhood picnic, at which you meet people you didn't know and "you have a wonderful time talking with them. You find out about them. They find out about you. It's not just a one-way conversation." Amy insists, "We *like* people."

Hanover Park Vineyard began with a trip to southern France in 1996. The Heltons were on their honeymoon, touring the countryside. Michael notes, "Before that trip, I had no opinion about wine one way or the other. I knew very little about wine." In France, however, "water was very expensive, and wine was very cheap. We had 23 days, and at the end of that period of time, I had a very definite opinion about wine. I loved it very much."

Noticing that the rolling hills of France were similar to those of the Piedmont, the Heltons began considering growing grapes and getting into the wine business. As Amy puts it, "You start to wonder what you'd like to do with your life." They spent weekends driving around the Yadkin Valley looking at property. Michael explains, "It was still part of the romance of continuing our honeymoon from France—taking leisurely drives and having a wonderful time." Most of the available tracts were either too large or too expensive—until they found a farmhouse on an affordable 23 acres. According to Michael, "at that moment, we both . . . hesitated. We thought, 'Wait a minute. Up to this point, it's been sort of a fantasy of speculation, without any thought of reality.' So we had to step back for a couple of days and really think about it." They talked it over with people. Amy says, "Some of our friends thought we were crazy. Other friends said, 'Go for it.' And obviously, we listened to those people."

Since they knew very little about growing grapes or making wine, the Heltons sought help. They took classes, searched the Internet, and talked to everyone they could. They contacted a

Michael and Amy Helton

grower in Virginia, Ed Schwab of Autumn Hill Vineyards, who im-
mediately invited them to spend the weekend. Amy remembers,
"When we were there that first time, he had to replace a few vines.
He took us out in the vineyards. He did one, he had Michael do
one, and he looked at me and said, 'You're getting into this, too.'
So we each planted a vine. The first of many vines I've planted."
Since then, Ed has become "a wonderful mentor and friend." They
return to his vineyards every year.

Michael also went to Westbend Vineyards and said, "I want to
volunteer." After talking with Steve Shepard, who was the winemaker
at the time, he was put to work. Michael recalls that "for three
solid days, I scrubbed tanks, I scrubbed gaskets, I scrubbed this and
that. My first reaction was, 'He just wants to see if I'm serious. This
weeds out the people that aren't.' I thought, 'I can handle that.' At
the end of the third day, I realized that what he was actually doing
was teaching me the golden rule of winemaking: Absolute fanati-
cism to cleanliness is the only way to be."

Initially, the Heltons planted two acres of vines. Later, they
learned that their neighbors had been watching them with curiosity. No one had ever grown grapes in the area, and people didn't
know what to make of these two schoolteachers who got their tractor stuck. Michael says, "I didn't know anything about farming. I
thought [the tractor] could go down through that stream and right

up the other side. . . . I was out plowing in the rain." What they lacked in experience, however, they made up for in energy. A friend later told the Heltons that people "couldn't figure out what you were doing or why you were doing it, but anybody that was working as hard as you do impressed the older people very much."

The neighbors were curious not only about the grapes, but about the restoration of the buildings as well. Constructed in 1897, the house had been abandoned since 1963. When the Heltons bought the property, the brambles and briars were so overgrown that it took a half-hour to walk the short distance from the barn to the house. Having made the decision to renovate, they spent 1999 working on the buildings. They took the barn apart and put it back together. As much as possible, they tried to stay true to the house's design and to reuse materials. When they ripped out the original flooring on the porch, they used the wood for shutters. The bar top in the tasting room was a shelf in the barn that they dried and restored. Michael and Amy admit that it's strange to look at photographs of the renovations. They can't believe the changes they've made and the amount of work they've done. Others can't either. Once the winery opened, people who once lived in the house began visiting and marveling at the restoration.

Although the Heltons love the space, it wasn't originally designed to be a winery, so they have had to make compromises. Michael admits, "The old house is nice, and I enjoy working in it, and it feels very comfortable, but there is a price to everything." The tasting room, for example, is sometimes too small for the number of visitors. At some point in the future, they may expand. Amy would like a sunroom. Michael wants a bigger barrel room. They even talk about putting up a new building. Whatever they do, however, they don't want to lose the intimate feel of the winery. Michael says, "I'm sure we'll grow, but as we get bigger and we have employees, I want them to help us in the vineyards. I want them to harvest and to be there when I'm pumping wine, so that any questions that they might be asked, they're knowledgeable about."

Hanover Park became the first bonded winery in Yadkin County since Prohibition. Local response has been positive. The chamber of commerce has honored the Heltons for their contributions to the community. Equally important to them are the informal tributes. Michael was working on a ladder one day when a group of bicyclists sped past and one shouted to another, "Have you tried this wine? It's Hanover Park, and it's excellent." Amy remembers one evening during the first year when they were walking through the fields. A father and daughter went by, and they couldn't see the Heltons in the vines. The daughter said, "Daddy, that's a lot of grapes," to which the father agreed. The child noted, "That's really pretty, isn't it?" and he answered, "Yes, dear, it's going to be beautiful."

Both Amy and Michael are artists, and it shows in their conversation. Amy often talks about the winery in terms of light and space. She believes that "there are many chemists that are winemakers, and yes, there's a science to it, but there is that something else. There is a certain art to doing it." Michael speaks of winemaking as problem solving: "On one level, it's alchemy. You're taking something of little value and making it of value. And you do the same with canvas. But it's also the process. When you're making art, you are discovering. . . . You're simultaneously discovering how to do the project. So discovery and knowledge are simultaneous as you're working your way through the project." The Heltons believe that, as with art, a person should make wine because he or she loves it. Michael insists, "You better have a passion for this because there are easier ways to make money."

The first years were financially difficult. Michael admits that "there were many times in the beginning that I was really worried, and [Amy] was just as calm as could be. Several times, she would say, 'Relax, relax.' At one point, she just had a conversation with me. She said, 'You make good wine. Don't worry about it. Stop driving yourself crazy.' " Amy knew they had a good product because, as she says, "I'm the one who watches people's faces in the tasting room." She came up with another method of reassuring her husband. As part of Michael's development as a winemaker, the Heltons regularly conduct blind tastings. Amy would put a bottle in a brown bag, and he would try a glass and then tell her every-thing he could about the wine. One night, she offered him "the mystery wine." Michael remembers, "I took a sip of it, and it was delightful, and I said, 'I hope someday I can make a wine this good. This would be all I want in life is to make something this good.' " They went into the kitchen, and Amy showed him the label: Hanover Park. Michael recalls, "I was shocked and elated. That's why I'm in this business. I get joy from it."

Hanover Park wines have already garnered acclaim. In particular, the Cabernet Sauvignon is becoming the winery's "flagship." The Heltons remember the first vintage they bottled. They had tasted it throughout the vinification process, and it had been "okay." Then, one afternoon, a wine seller told them, "Your whites are wonderful, comparable to anything in California, but I want a good, full-bodied red." They decided to have him try the Cabernet Sauvignon. They poured and tasted it. In the silence that followed, everyone in the room looked at one another. Michael says, "The magical gnome had gotten into the wine and done things to it. I was shocked. It had a nose, character, a fruit flavor that it had never had before." The Heltons knew that they had something special. This was confirmed later when Michael offered the Cabernet Sauvignon to another person in the wine industry, who was "astounded." The two men went into the barrel room and started to experiment and blend. At one point, the man turned to Michael and said, "You've just discovered some magic." He urged the Heltons to plant more of the varietal: "This doesn't happen normally. There's a rare combination that you've got here. There's something that's working. Stay with it."

The Heltons have every intention of staying with it. It is ironic, however, that after their trip to France, they have rarely managed to take vacations. Now, honeymooners come to them. So do others. Friends, students, and customers come not only to taste but to pick grapes during harvest or to bottle. Amy marvels at the "interesting assortment" of people who arrive to help: "You never can tell who is going to show up." One couple who were simply visiting friends stayed for hours after their friends left because the woman loved helping in the winery. Michael says, "It's really quite nice. We're giving to people, and they're giving to us."

Hanover Park Vineyard Wine List

Whites
Barrel Fermented Chardonnay, Chardonnay, Viognier

Rosé
Hanover Park Rosé

Reds
Cabernet Franc, Cabernet Sauvignon, Chambourcin, Mourvedre

Recipe Suggestion from Hanover Park Vineyard

Poached Pears

1 cup sugar
2 cups Hanover Park Chambourcin

1 vanilla bean
6 ripe Bosc, Barlett, or Anjou pears

In a saucepan large enough to hold the pears, combine the sugar and wine. Slit vanilla bean and add to wine mixture. Bring to a boil, then simmer. Halve, peel, and core pears. Add pears to simmering liquid. When pears are tender, remove with a slotted spoon to a bowl. Reduce liquid to a syrup. Pour syrup over pear halves, cool, cover, and refrigerate until ready to eat. Serve alone or with vanilla ice cream.

Profile: Old North State Winegrowers Cooperative

Wade Nichols, Rooster Ridge Vineyards

On August 8, 2002, Fred Jones, president of the Old North State Winegrowers Cooperative, stood in an abandoned department store in downtown Mount Airy holding a check for over a quarter of a million dollars. He smiled at the crowd of farmers and government officials from county, state, and federal agencies. They smiled back. The check represented two grants from the United States Department of Agriculture's Rural Development Program and the Appalachian Regional Commission, given to help the co-op transform the building into a winery. Once the winery is completed, it will provide a market for co-op members, train people for the industry, and, according to Jones, be a "business incubator" from which "will spring 15 to 20 more wineries."

The co-op began in 2001. Several people who were interested in growing grapes and becoming involved in the wine industry decided to overcome a lack of financial capital and experience by putting their resources together. One of the group's founding members, Wade Nichols of Rooster Ridge Vineyards, helped write the co-op's charter. "I thought that we'd probably get about 10 to 12 members to sign up," he says. "The very first day, we had 21, and within a week's time, we had 27." Now, the Old North State Winegrowers Cooperative includes 50 farmers from counties across the state, and Fred Jones anticipates that in the near future, members will have planted over 250 acres of vines. Consequently, the co-op, Jones says, "will be the largest winery in the South."

Nichols is confident about the organization's prospects. He believes that "if we work hard, we can be a part of defining what is unique about North Carolina wine and Yadkin Valley wine." Although he admits that some people dismiss cooperatives as cumbersome and difficult to manage, he points out that such ventures are common in the European wine trade. Furthermore, farmers are used to them. He says, "Growing up, my family was a part of agricultural cooperatives. Our phone system was a co-op, our electrical system was a co-op, so I knew that if those co-ops have been around providing service for 70 years, we can have a successful wine co-op as well." The key is that people work together, and so far they have. Members come from a wide variety of backgrounds, including farming, retail, public relations, law, construction, food service, and accounting. As a result, everyone has something useful to contribute. Nichols laughs, "Meetings are never dull."

As they searched for a location for the winery, co-op board members reviewed numerous sites in rural counties. Eventually, they chose Mount Airy, in part because the town has a documented 300,000 visitors a year. The choice pleased Nichols. He says, "I like the idea of bringing the farm back into Mount Airy. When I was a kid, I lived about five miles outside of town, and the farm economy still had quite a bit of influence here. We've seen that diminish over the years, but this is a way of bringing it back in. I like that we're the ones that are going to create new jobs."

The Mount Airy winery, scheduled to open in the summer of 2003, will produce wine under the Carolina Harvest label. Eventually, the co-op would also like the building to include a restaurant, meeting rooms, and perhaps even a culinary school. Nichols admits, "We're big dreamers, and so far we've actually seen some of our dreams come true."

Old North State Winery

_R_agApple Lassie Vineyards

3720 Rockford Road
Boonville, N.C. 27011
Phone: 866-RAG-APPLE
Website: www.ragapplelassie.com
E-mail: info@RagAppleLassie.com
Hours: Wednesday-Sunday, noon-6 P.M.
Tasting-room fee: none

Owners: Frank and Lenna Hobson
Winemaker: Linda King
First vines planted: 2000
First year as bonded winery: 2002
First wine release: 2002

Directions: From Interstate 77, go east on N.C. 67. Three miles east of Boonville, turn south at the Rockford Road intersection. The winery is on the left. From U.S. 421, take U.S. 601 North. Turn east on N.C. 67 at Boonville and go 3 miles. Turn south at the Rockford Road intersection. The winery is on the left. From U.S. 52, go west on N.C. 67 to the Rockford Road intersection. Turn south. The winery is on the left.

Lenna Hobson calls her husband, Frank, "the quintessential farmer." She says, "He has a farming heritage, but he also loves farming. He's a farmer to his toenails." Years ago, when Frank worked for a fertilizer company and was told that he had to quit farming and concentrate on running its stores, he quit the company instead. For most of his life, Frank has grown tobacco, but in the 1990s, as the government steadily reduced his allotment, he began looking for a new crop. His choice was a "process of elimination," Frank says. "I don't like chickens. The neighbors don't like hogs. And I've run all the cows and pasture that I'm going to run." Lenna laughs, "He said he didn't want anything you had to feed that would get out when you wanted to go somewhere on a Saturday night." Intrigued by the development of Shelton Vineyards, the Hobsons visited it several times. One evening, Frank said, "Well, why don't we plant grapes, then?" It was, Lenna remembers, like a light bulb clicking on. Now, visitors to RagApple Lassie Vineyards can see rows of tobacco growing next to acres of grapes. It's a symbolic juxtaposition of what some consider to be the Yadkin Valley's past and future.

Frank says, "The vineyard business has been our salvation here," but the Hobsons did not jump into the industry rashly. They methodically educated themselves, planned, and moved ahead in stages. First, Frank, who also co-owns a farm supply store, began making calls and doing research. In the process, he discovered that "there are very few suppliers of everything you need in the vineyard business except on the West Coast." So he expanded his business to supply poles, equipment, and chemicals to the area's grape growers. He also planted his own vines. Lenna says, "At first, it's all so overwhelming because it's so totally brand-new. You're not sure what's required." But after going through a year's cycle, they realized that grape growing "dovetails nicely with the other farming operations." They decided to take the next step and build a winery.

When the University of North Carolina at Charlotte's School of Design heard about the Hobsons' intentions, it asked if the winery could be used as a design project for the senior class. Students came to the area several times, interviewed Frank and Lenna, walked the property, and came up with different concepts. During the process, the Hobsons learned that the professor, Greg Snyder, did private commissions. When they approached him to be the architect, he agreed. His design situated the winery where it could take advantage of views of Pilot Mountain and also be next to a natural amphitheater where musical events could be held. A silo with a circular stairway to the barrel room was to offer an architectural reference to the area's farming heritage. The event room, designed to seat approximately 270 people, was to open on to a covered terrace. The Hobsons loved the design. Before beginning construction, however, they went to Napa Valley to meet a winery consultant. They knew "textbook theory" but wanted to talk to someone about the practical aspects of the building. Lenna says, "He showed us nuances of what makes the workspace of a winery a nightmare and what makes it a dream. It's as simple as sloping the floor so that the water runs towards the drain, and that way, you don't have to squeegee it."

To counterbalance their inexperience, the Hobsons knew they wanted a veteran winemaker. Impressed with her work at the largest estate winery in Ohio and her education at the University of California at Davis, they hired Linda King. Both she and the Hobsons believe blends will be an important part of the winery. Lenna explains, "Our niche might be doing some interesting Meritages. When there are a hundred world-class Chardonnays or Cabernets, until your vines are very mature and you are very good at what you do, it's hard to stand out against those. But we can take a good Chardonnay or Cabernet and make some very interesting blends that are uniquely ours because of the blend and because of the soil." Since the farm is located in the "Old Belt" tobacco region, an area that provides some of the sweetest, most highly prized tobacco on the market, the Hobsons believe the soil will also produce grapes that are equally prized and distinctive.

For its initial releases, RagApple Lassie offered wines that were custom-crushed by RayLen's winemaker, Steve Shepard. To Lenna, the experience with this first wine was a sign that she and Frank were in the right business. Once they had a harvest, the Hobsons needed French oak barrels, but no one believed they could get them in time. The barrels come from two different French forests (depending on whether they will be used for white or red wine), and they must be ordered and paid for a year in advance. Frank called a company in France and explained the situation. In less than a month,

Lenna and Frank Hobson of RagApple Lassie Vineyard

the barrels arrived. He says, "They shipped just exactly what we needed." The bill came later. Meanwhile, other wineries were still waiting for orders that they had paid for months earlier. Lenna says, "I viewed that as a sign that we're exactly where we're supposed to be, doing what we're supposed to be doing."

Besides acquiring the first barrels, the easiest part of establishing the vineyards was choosing the name. As a teenager, Frank had a Grand Champion Holstein named RagApple Lassie. Even now, decades later, he talks fondly about carrying alfalfa pellets in his pockets and having RagApple Lassie come running to him and stick her nose in his clothes. She was, Frank says, "a big pet." Consequently, the winery's website explains, "the opportunity to combine the farm heritage of Frank's life, with a name that was both unique and memorable made 'RagApple Lassie' the obvious choice." A photograph of RagApple Lassie (and a young Frank) can be seen in the winery. She also is prominently featured in the winery's marketing, from its logo to its website.

In fact, if Frank is "the quintessential farmer," then Lenna might be "the model marketer." Promotional ideas pour from her. Before its first wine release, Lenna decided the winery needed a product, so she arranged to have RagApple Lassie Bottled Water available at events. In October 2001, she organized "A Celebration of Firsts," which was, she explains, "the first annual vineyard party celebrating the first year's growth of the first year's planting of the first Boonville vineyard on the first Saturday of October at the first minute after four." It was also a charity event. Habitat for Humanity brought two-by-fours that were to be used in its next house, which guests could sign with a donation. The party raised $6,000. In the future, in addition to hosting parties and other events, Lenna would like to institute an "Adopt-A-Vine" program at the vineyards; people who make donations to Habitat for Humanity will be able to choose a varietal and vine that will be "theirs," complete with plaque.

The Hobsons have enjoyed establishing RagApple Lassie. Although it has involved "stomach-turning investment decisions," Lenna insists that "it's been exhilarating and great fun. There has never been a day that we haven't considered it fun and fascinating." They also have discovered an unexpected social phenomenon. When they travel, people respond very differently if they say they own a vineyard instead of a tobacco farm. Lenna says the reaction is astounding; people's eyes open wide, they ask numerous questions, and they seem fascinated. No one, Lenna laughs, treats them like this when they present themselves as "farmers." Yet farmers are proudly what Frank and Lenna are. The romantic view of vineyards amuses them because it ignores the hard work involved in growing grapes. In fact, Lenna says, "if we had a surprise, it was that [grapes are] as labor-intensive as tobacco. Tobacco is labor-intensive three or four months. Vineyards are labor-intensive year-round."

Despite their 26 acres of grapes, Lenna and Frank insist that, for now, "tobacco pays the bills" and that they will grow it as long as there is a market. But for their grandchildren, who they think are the ones "who are really going to benefit and who are really going to have the opportunity to do neat things with [the winery]," things might be different. What pays the bills for future generations of Hobsons may be the vines that Frank and Lenna are planting now.

RagApple Lassie Vineyards Wine List

Whites
Boonville Blanc, Chardonnay

Red
Cabernet Sauvignon

Coming soon
Cabernet Franc, Merlot, Syrah, Viognier

RagApple Lassie Vineyard

Recommended Pairings from RagApple Lassie Vineyards

Cabernet Sauvignon with duck, veal, pasta, or beef

Boonville Blanc with cheesecake, soft, buttery cheeses, or very ripe fruit

Recipe Suggestion from RagApple Lassie Vineyards

Veal Cordon Bleu

½-pound veal round steak or cutlet, cut ¼ inch thick
2 thin slices boiled ham
2 slices Swiss cheese
2 tablespoons flour

1 egg, beaten slightly
½ cup Italian breadcrumbs
2 tablespoons butter
2 teaspoons or more RagApple Lassie Chardonnay

Cut veal into 4 equal pieces and pound until very thin. Cut ham and cheese smaller than veal pieces. Top 2 veal pieces with ham and cheese, then place remaining veal pieces on top of cheese. Press edges together and seal them. Dip in flour, then egg, then breadcrumbs. Melt butter in a skillet. Brown meat over medium heat until golden. Remove to a warm platter. Stir wine into skillet. Spoon mixture over meat. Serve with either RagApple Lassie Chardonnay or RagApple Lassie Cabernet Sauvignon. Serves 2.

RayLen Vineyards

3577 U.S. 158
Mocksville, N.C. 27028
Phone and fax: 336-998-3100
Website: www.RayLenvineyards.com
On-line ordering available
E-mail: info@RayLenvineyards.com
Hours: Monday-Saturday, 11 A.M.-6 P.M.
Tasting-room fee: $3

Owners: Joe and Joyce Neely
Winemaker: Steve Shepard
First vines planted: 1999
First year as bonded winery: 2000
First wine release: 2001

Directions: From Interstate 40 West, take the exit for N.C.
801 and drive south. Go right on U.S. 158 West. The winery
is on the right after 4 miles. From Interstate 40 East, take
the exit for Farmington Road. Turn left at the stop sign on to
U.S. 158 East. The winery is on the left after 2 miles.

In the late 1990s, Joe Neely considered the prospects of the North
Carolina wine industry and liked what he saw. In fact, he liked the
prospects so much that, although he was supposedly retired, he
couldn't resist getting involved. Inspired by trips to Napa Valley
with Lee and Janet Martin and George and Susan Little of Round

RayLen Vineyards winemaker Steve Shepard

Peak Vineyards and with Marilyn Thomer of Parducci Winery, Joe and his wife, Joyce, planted six acres of vineyards in Lewisville. Then, encouraged by their friends Ed and Charlie Shelton, the owners of Shelton Vineyards, they decided to establish their own winery. They bought a 115-acre dairy farm, began planting vines, and built a showcase winery that they named RayLen, a combination of their daughters' names, Rachel and Len.

Because Joe had been involved with a number of successful entrepreneurial start-ups, the Neelys had confidence in their business plan, which suggested that a winery with a capacity of 20,000 cases could be reasonably profitable. They chose the land because of its location in the Yadkin Valley, a fertile grape-growing region, and its proximity to Interstate 40. Their smartest business decision, however, may have been hiring Steve Shepard as RayLen's winemaker and general manager. When the Neelys offered him the chance to be involved, Steve, known for his award-winning work at Westbend Vineyards, couldn't resist. He says, "I decided to jump on board and start all over again. I really like the challenge of starting with nothing and building it up."

For Steve, it was a chance to create an ideal winery. Working with architect Ray Troxell and others involved in the design of Shelton Vineyards, he helped plan RayLen's physical layout, including the crucial placement of tanks, water lines, and electrical lines. He ordered state-of-the-art equipment ranging from a computerized European press to a portable water heater that produces a high-volume spray of scalding water for cleaning. Steve says, "I've been making wine for 25 years, and I've done four or five different wineries. I took the best of everything from those other wineries and put in everything I could think of here." When RayLen began production, Steve found that the winery worked "like a dream." At 11,000 square feet, it was designed for growth. The plan is to double production each year until the winery reaches its capacity.

Steve also has had a free hand in developing the wines. Pointing out that "different winemakers have different styles," he says, "I like wines that are high in acid. They go better with foods. . . . I like something that's going to wake up your taste buds." He doesn't, however, try to please only himself; his goal is "to make wines that people enjoy drinking." Steve insists that winemaking is an art, and that a winemaker should therefore have an artistic sensibility and a sense of personal style. But he or she also needs to consider audience tastes. There must be a balance as a winemaker tries "to develop something that's really creative" and also a wine "that people are going to go head over heels over."

In RayLen's first years, Steve has concentrated on Chardonnay, Viognier, Merlot, Shiraz, and Bordeaux varietals. Although RayLen's 40 acres of vineyards eventually will supply most of the winery's needs, Steve also works with other North Carolina growers. For years, he has bought crops from Larry Kehoe's Silver Creek Vineyards, and he makes a Chardonnay exclusively with Silver Creek grapes. Kehoe, a longtime wine enthusiast, praises the result because he feels "it's not a California style—that pineapple juice with oak logs floating in it. It's much more French." Steve also likes working with Shiraz, which he believes may become a key varietal in North Carolina's future. It grows well here and has interesting qualities, including a "nice jammy character." In addition to featuring Shiraz in a vintage wine, he uses it in Carolinius, a special blend he has created for RayLen. Showcasing three Bordeaux reds—Merlot, Cabernet Sauvignon, and Cabernet Franc—Carolinius met with immediate success. Its first release quickly sold out.

RayLen's wines have already garnered acclaim. For example, every one of its initial 2000 releases earned medals in competitions. In fact, Joe says that "if I had known that the wines were going to be as good as they were, I would have gone a lot faster. We've been extremely pleased with them." Still, he admits that in the first year, some of RayLen's best customers were a couple who bought as many hats and shirts as they did bottles of wine. When asked why they found these items so appealing, they explained that their names were Ray and Lynne.

Visitors to RayLen are encouraged to bring picnics. The tasting room has tables and chairs, and its windows provide views of the vineyards' rolling hills. The building also features a wraparound porch with rocking chairs for relaxing. Occasionally, RayLen sponsors events, such as a clambake to celebrate the release of the 2001 Carolinius. Its large second floor can be reserved for private business meetings.

In addition to its wines and clothing products, RayLen's tasting room displays for purchase several pieces of handcrafted furniture, wooden boxes, and other pieces of woodwork. These are the products of another business with which Joe is involved—or, as he puts it, "another one of my dabblings." Although he insists that "I'm trying to stay retired," he hasn't been very successful in his attempt. In the future, this may only get worse. The more prosperous RayLen becomes, the more difficult staying retired is likely to be for Joe.

RayLen Vineyards

RayLen Vineyards Wine List

 ## Whites
Chardonnay, Silver Creek Vineyards Chardonnay, Viognier

 ## Reds
Cabernet Franc, Carolinius, Merlot, Shiraz

Recommended Pairings from RayLen Vineyards

Carolinius with any favorite dish or appetizer

Silver Creek Vineyards Chardonnay with seafood, pork, or chicken

Merlot or Cabernet Franc with beef, lamb, or pasta

Shiraz with appetizers, pasta, or spicy Thai dishes

Viognier with broiled shellfish, veal, or poultry

Profile: Steve Shepard, Winemaker, RayLen Vineyards

Steve Shepard

Talk long enough to someone in the North Carolina wine industry and you'll hear Steve Shepard's name. Not only has he created some of the state's most noted wines, but for almost 15 years, he has played a pivotal role in the industry's development by generously sharing his expertise, time, and energy. As one winemaker puts it, "Steve gives advice freely. He doesn't mind telling you if your wine isn't right, and he'll tell you what to do to make it better."

Ironically, if Shepard had followed his original career path, people would be asking for advice about their own heath, rather than about the health of their vines. He began college as a premed student, but after a year, "I was kind of bored with it," Shepard says. Since his college had a strong agricultural curriculum, he decided to try horticulture.

Early in the program, Shepard took a laboratory course during which students were responsible for pruning a section of apple orchard. He remembers, "Of course, it's February in Pennsylvania, and we're up in this tree, and I'm reaching across with these loppers, trying to prune these branches off, and they're icy, and it's drizzly rain and cold, and I thought to myself, 'Man, I don't want to do this with the rest of my life. This isn't what I had in mind.' " Nevertheless, Shepard continued his studies. In his junior year, he began taking courses in small-fruit culture, such as berries and grapes. For another laboratory course, he was responsible for pruning part of a vineyard: "It was February again, and I was out there, and I had these little hand clippers in my hand, and I was standing on the ground, pruning away, and I'm going, 'Now, this isn't too bad. I think I can handle this.' " Shepard took some food-science courses, including one on winemaking. He realized, "You've got the grapes, you've got the wine—these things seem to go hand in hand." He had found his career.

The summer after his junior year, Shepard headed to California with $150. He hitchhiked through Napa Valley, staying in campsites, visiting wineries, and "sponging up as much as I could." Although he wanted to stay and find a job, he knew "my parents would have killed me." So he returned for his final year of college. After graduation, he started at the bottom of the Pennsylvania wine industry, putting capsules on bottles and cleaning tanks. Eventually, he worked his way up to a winemaker position. In 1989, Shepard joined North Carolina's Westbend Vineyards, where he helped prove that high-quality European-style wines could be made in the area. Then, in 2000, looking for a new challenge, he helped establish RayLen Vineyards.

Although Shepard has won numerous awards during his career, he doesn't emphasize them. He insists, "Winning medals and awards is part of your job. You should win them. If you're not winning awards, then you've got a problem."

He loves winemaking because it's never boring. He says, "You're doing something that's going to be a little bit different every year, and you're going to have different challenges." He also appreciates the constant opportunity to improve his work. As a winemaker, "you always get a second chance," he says. "You get more than a second chance. You get a chance every new vintage."

Shelton Vineyards

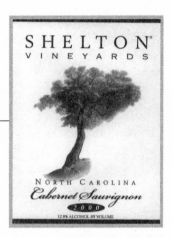

286 Cabernet Lane
Dobson, N.C. 27017
Phone: 336-366-4724
Website: www.sheltonvineyards.com
On-line ordering available
E-mail: sales@sheltonvineyards.com
Hours: Monday-Saturday, 10 A.M.-6 P.M.; Sunday, 1-6 P.M.
Tasting-room fee: The $5 fee includes tastings, a tour, and a souvenir
    glass.

Owners: Charles M. and R. Edwin Shelton
Winemaker: Matt Dyar
First vines planted: 1999
First year as bonded winery: 2000
First wine release: 2000

Directions: From Interstate 77, take Exit 93 (the Dobson exit). Turn
right, then take the first right on to Twin Oaks Road. The winery's
entrance is on the right after 2.5 miles. From Interstate 74, take U.S.
601 to Dobson and follow the signs.

According to Charlie Shelton, the origins of Shelton Vineyards
were an impulse buy and a late-night television commercial. In 1994,
Charlie bought an old dairy farm at an auction. He had no plans
for it. "I just thought," he says, "that we ought to own a farm." After
a few years, he and his brother and business partner, Ed, began to
seriously ask, "What can we do with this land? What can we do to

help some of the people's thinking in this county that there's other things that you can do besides tobacco?" Then, one night, as he watched the NIT basketball finals, Charlie saw a promotion for the viticulture program at the University of California at Davis. He called the school to get information about growing grapes. Someone at the school referred him to someone at Virginia Tech, who referred him to someone else, who referred him to someone else. Charlie persisted. Eventually, he made contact with a consultant in Tryon, North Carolina, who visited the farm, tested the soil, reviewed the climate, and pronounced it a good place to grow grapes.

After the Sheltons decided to establish vineyards, they went, as one friend puts it, "about 90 miles an hour." In 1999, they planted European varietals on 60 acres. Each year, they expanded, until by 2001 the vineyards covered nearly 200 acres and included 14 different varietals.

To design the 33,000-square-foot winery, Charlie and Ed convinced North Carolina architect Ray Troxell, an old friend and business associate, to come out of retirement. Troxell has enjoyed working with the brothers and their construction company, Shelco, Inc. He says, "Charlie and Ed are most unusual people. They are the salt of the earth, in my book." He appreciated that the brothers "were not interested in budget work. They wanted first-class. They always do, and they always get it. I think that job probably went as smoothly as any job they ever built."

Believing that if, as Charlie puts it, "you've got the right people and the right equipment, it will make the right wine," the Sheltons hired industry experts, including general manager Sean McRitchie from Oregon's Willamette Valley. And they outfitted the winery with top-of-the-line equipment. McRitchie says that the Sheltons told him, " 'We want to do it right. If it improves the wine even a little bit, let's do it.' " For example, they decided to incorporate a gravity-flow system that requires minimal pumping of wine. The effort paid off. With its first releases, Shelton Vineyards began winning awards.

The brothers insist that they didn't create the state-of-the-art

Left: Charlie Shelton, above: Ed Shelton
of Shelton Vineyards

winery simply as a business venture. They also intended "to make a statement." They wanted to demonstrate the land's possibilities. In an area that has increasingly lost jobs due to changes in the tobacco, textile, and furniture industries, finding new sources of revenue is crucial. The Sheltons believe that one of these sources may be grapes. According to Charlie, a survey done by researchers at Virginia Tech found that almost 95 percent of Surry County is ideal for growing vinifera. Part of the Yadkin Valley, it has a good climate—warm summers and mild winters—fertile soil, and rolling hills, which provide drainage. Shelton Vineyards, then, serves as a model to area farmers of what can be done.

Having been born and raised in the North Carolina Piedmont, the Sheltons repeatedly emphasize their desire to give something back to the community. Charlie says of the winery, "The most rewarding thing is to see what it has done for Surry County—in particular, this area, Mount Airy. It's sort of put a new breath of life in these folks." At one time, the Mount Airy region had a significant tourism industry, and the Sheltons believe that this can be rebuilt. Ed remarks, "I'd love to see a hundred wineries up here in this area. I'd like to see people doing things that use the land. I think that rural North Carolina has got to develop its rural character." To that end, the brothers intend Shelton Vineyards to be a "destination area." Larry Kehoe, the owner of Silver Creek Vineyards, believes they have succeeded. He says of the Sheltons, "What they've done is so magnificent. You drive down that lane and suddenly say, 'My God, I'm in Napa Valley.' It's amazing."

The winery has a 50,000-case production capacity. Tours for visitors were planned as part of the building's layout. Consequently, as Troxell points out, "the public can walk through this facility and see the different operations and not interfere with them and yet have a very comfortable path." Organized tours run at regular intervals. Large windows offer views of the various work areas, such as the bottling and fermentation rooms. The tasting room is a large, beautiful space with a three-story atrium lit by an enormous chandelier. The gift shop offers a variety of items for sale.

Outside, the wraparound porch has rocking chairs situated to overlook some of the vineyards. Troxell says, "The vistas and views of that land are magnificent. That was an integral part of the design." The grounds include picnic areas and a small pond. Shelton often hosts concerts and festival events. In 2001, to complement the winery, the brothers opened Shelton Cheeses on the property, a facility that makes handcrafted cheeses from goat and Jersey cow milk processed by a local dairy. To complete the pastoral setting, two dogs—a black and a yellow Labrador named Cabernet and Chardonnay—roam the property.

The brothers set out to make a statement, and they have. Their impact on the state's wine industry has been enormous. Their example has convinced other farmers to grow grapes; many of those farmers now belong to the Old North State Winegrowers Cooperative. The Sheltons have also helped inspire the development of several wineries, among them RayLen and RagApple Lassie. They sponsored the application for an official designation that would make the Yadkin Valley an "appellation," a distinct winegrowing region. In 1998, they started a viticulture and oenology program at Surry Community College, the only such degree program on the

East Coast. They also funded the program for its first two years. Shelton Vineyards itself serves as a type of educational institution. Sean McRitchie says it is "a great research facility," thanks to its multiple clonings of vines, multiple rootstocks, and size. According to one small winery owner, the brothers' political and business clout has allowed them "to open doors a lot of us have been hammering on for years."

The Sheltons are leaving a legacy not only for their community, but also, they hope, for their own families. In a variety of ways, Shelton Vineyards pays tribute to both their ancestors and their descendants. The red-wine blend Madison Lee is named after their grandfathers. A trophy case visible on the tour displays photographs of the brothers' lives, families, and careers. The winery's design of five *S*'s represents the five children who someday will inherit Shelton Vineyards. In fact, when the winery opened, Ed stated that "at Shelton Vineyards, we are creating a place that will soon produce the best wine on the East Coast. After that, it will be our children's responsibility to make it the best wine in the United States. And after that, it will be up to our grandchildren to make it the best in the world." The sentiment suggests how much rural North Carolina and its families have changed. After all, Ed and Charlie grew up in a family of teetotalers and were hesitant to explain to their 93-year-old father that they were going into the wine business. Once they finally did so, their father thought for a moment and then said, according to Charlie, " 'Well, the old folks used to eat a little vinegar with their food to help digestion, and I think wine is vinegar, so you'll be all right.' "

Shelton Vineyards Wine List

 ### Whites
Barrel Fermented Chardonnay, Madison Lee White, Viognier

Rosé
Salem Fork Blush

Reds
Cabernet Sauvignon, Madison Lee Red, Merlot, Salem Fork Zephyr Red, Syrah

Recommended Pairing from Shelton Vineyards

Chardonnay with ravioli and a creamy pesto sauce; those who make their own pasta can stuff the ravioli with Shelton Sun-Dried Tomato Chevre.

Recipe Suggestion from Shelton Vineyards

Baked Vidalia Onion with Cheddar Cheese

1 Vidalia onion
2 tablespoons olive oil
pinch of salt

pinch of pepper
1 cup Shelton Cheddar Cheese, shredded

Quarter and open onion. Drizzle with olive oil and sprinkle with salt, pepper, and cheese. Bake 10 minutes at 400 degrees. Serve with Shelton Vineyards Cabernet Sauvignon.

Profile: Ray Troxell, Architect, Shelton Vineyards and RayLen Vineyards

Ray Troxell

In sixth grade, Ray Troxell was asked what he wanted to be when he grew up. He said he wanted to be an architect, and that's exactly what he became. Still, he was surprised when Ed and Charlie Shelton phoned in January 1998 and said, "We're going to build a winery, and we're calling all our old friends to work on it. Are you interested in helping?" For one, Troxell was retired. Then there was the fact that he had not only never designed a winery but had never even been in one. The Sheltons, however, value long-term relationships and loyalty. Since Troxell had designed their first building—in King, North Carolina—they thought he was the right choice.

Troxell says he was excited by the project because "it was just a great, great opportunity to learn something new." The Sheltons took him to California on a tour of Napa Valley wineries and arranged meetings with industry engineers. After he learned the mechanics of winemaking, he began drawing up plans. The result, Shelton Vineyards, "turned out quite well," he believes. At least, he says with a laugh, no one who works there has complained.

After completing Shelton Vineyards, Troxell found himself with more work. Joe Neely asked for his help with RayLen Vineyards. There, he did more than just design the building. In exchange for a bottle of Chardonnay, he agreed to paint a watercolor for the RayLen label. Then Troxell was called again by the Sheltons, who wanted him to design a cheese shop for the vineyards' grounds.

Designing wineries is the latest phase of a 40-year career during which Troxell has worked on everything from nursing homes to secret government

Shelton Vineyards

bunkers. After graduating from the University of Illinois in 1950, he served in the United States Air Force, where, as an air installation officer, he helped plan for both the immediate needs of bases and their future growth. After his discharge in 1953, he took a job in Washington as a general contractor because he thought that, "as an architect, it would be fantastic experience" and a chance to learn firsthand about the construction industry.

In Washington, Troxell had one particularly memorable job: "One of our projects was to remodel a four-story building in the middle of a mountain." Everyone working there had to have special clearance. Troxell says, "If you wanted to go to the bathroom, you could, but there was a guy with a machine gun behind you all the way," and as you went down the corridors, you could not look left or right. He remembers, "Nobody could know where the entrance was, until one day I opened up the *U.S. News & World Report*, and there was a picture of the damn entrance."

Eventually, Troxell moved to Winston-Salem, where he worked for Larson and Larson, Architects, and helped design buildings on the Wake Forest University campus. In 1962, he established his own firm specializing in health-care facilities. No matter what the project, Troxell believes that an architect's job consists of two fundamental skills: "Architecture is planning, and architecture is problem solving. If it doesn't have those two elements and doesn't satisfy the client, I don't care how pretty it is, it's a failure."

The Shelton and RayLen wineries satisfied their clients. Troxell says, "I'm really proud of both of them." For now, he is retired again, but if the phone rings with another winery project, he admits that he would probably take it. It would be a chance to keep learning, and, he says, "I do love the work."

SilkHope Winery

2601 Silk Hope Gum Springs Road
Pittsboro, N.C. 27312
Phone: 919-742-4601
E-mail: Wallybutler@Pinehurst.net
Hours: by appointment
Tasting-room fee: none

Owner: Wally Butler
Winemaker: Wally Butler
First vines planted: 1985
First year as bonded winery: 2000
First wine release: 2001

Directions: From Pittsboro, go 4 miles north on N.C. 87, then turn left on Silk Hope Gum Springs Road. The winery is on the left after 2.5 miles, approximately 300 yards past Emmaus Church.

In the 1980s, *Wally Butler,* a forester, bought several acres of land in Chatham County because he liked its timber prospects. At 700 feet in elevation, it also had beautiful views of the surrounding countryside. Wally remembers, "I stood up on the hill and looked at this little church down there in the valley, and I thought, 'Man, that's a sweet place to plant grapes.' " It was an ironic thought since, several years earlier, he had been adamant about the impossibility of growing grapes in the area. In the late 1970s, Wally had appraised timber for a man named David Reed, who was clearing his

Wally Butler of SilkHope Winery

land to plant vinifera vines. Wally had been skeptical: "I said, 'No, that will never work. You can't grow those kind of grapes around here.'" Reed proved him wrong, and the two men formed a friendship. Later, Wally even bought grapes from him to make wine.

Inspired by Reed's success and the possibilities of his own land, Wally planted a small number of vines in 1985. He dabbled with them for a few years but admits, "I didn't care for them just right." Then he decided to get more serious. He joined the North Carolina Winegrower's Association, sought advice, and planted more vines. Now, he has two vineyards: one for white varietals such as Seyval Blanc and one for reds such as Chambourcin.

As Wally began putting significant effort into grape growing, he also became more serious about his winemaking. He had been a hobbyist for years. "I started making wine because I like to drink wine," he says. After he made the decision to pursue the business commercially, he founded SilkHope Winery.

SilkHope is a small operation. Wally says, "I'm very basic. . . . I don't have any pumps or anything like that." Using a small stainless-steel tank and seven barrels of American oak, he usually produces only a couple thousand bottles a year. In 2001, for example, SilkHope released 250 cases. Everything is done by hand, including putting on the labels. These feature the family crest. Wally says with a smile, "My mother insisted that I put it on."

Although Wally's mother isn't much of a wine drinker, she does like scuppernong and sweet wines, so Wally makes batches of these occasionally. As a winemaker, however, he prefers to work with reds. He admits, "I always wind up, when I'm drinking white, saying, 'You know, this stuff isn't too bad.' . . . Reds, that's my thing." His 2000 Chambourcin earned a medal at the 2001 North Carolina State Fair, and for Wally, the award represented validation for years of effort.

Wally runs SilkHope from a small metal hangar and a small green sheet-metal building that contains a walk-in cooler for controlled-environment fermenting. Although he acknowledges these no-frills buildings are poorly designed for his purposes, he chose them for a simple reason: affordability. The expense of establishing a winery surprised Wally, who notes that "it's depressing to do taxes." He says, "I thought I realized how much money it would be and how much work it would take, but I didn't." Eventually, he would like to build a winery that has more appeal to visitors, but for now, all the money goes into the grapes.

Wally has had problems finding reliable help. Because he works full-time himself, tending his two acres of vines can be a daunting task. In 2002, it became even more difficult when he discovered that Pierce's disease had attacked a large portion of his vineyards. A bacteria that devastates grapevines, Pierce's disease is believed by scientists to be spread by different hosts, including insects called "sharpshooters." It exists only in mild climates and can go undetected for a long time. Wally points out that the vines look good in the early stages of infection, but then, within a season, they can be dead.

The disease reduced SilkHope's crop yield by two-thirds. As a result, the winery's production declined to less than a hundred cases. Wally notes ruefully, "I at least have the satisfaction of being the first place in Chatham County to be diagnosed with Pierce's disease." He is working with researchers at the nearby universities to determine what should be done. He may replant many of his vines, or he may concentrate on growing the varietal Norton, since it seems to have a high resistance to Pierce's disease.

Wally is determined to keep SilkHope Winery going. He hopes that the worst is over. He says, "I've already had my pride hurt and gotten over that, so now I just have to see what happens." In the future, he is determined not to let the work and expense overwhelm him. He insists, "I'm going to be a little more laid-back and just take it as it comes."

SilkHope Winery Wine List

Whites
Seyval Blanc, Vidal Blanc, Villard Blanc

Red
Chambourcin

Recommended Pairings from SilkHope Winery

Chambourcin with sliced Parmesan cheese, sautéed chilies, onions, and tortilla chips

Chambourcin with a Hershey's chocolate bar; Wally Butler notes, "It sounds crazy, I know, but the hint of chocolate and the natural richness of the wine mingle with those same qualities of the chocolate bar and deliver pleasures unknown to those who haven't tried it."

$\mathcal{W}$estbend Vineyards

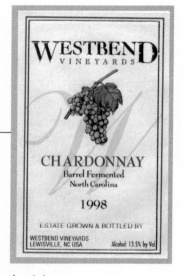

5394 Williams Road
Lewisville, N.C. 27023
Phone: 877-901-5032 or 336-945-5032
Fax: 336-945-5294
Website: www.westbendvineyards.com
E-mail: info@westbendvineyards.com
Hours: Tuesday-Saturday, 11 A.M.-6 P.M.; Sunday, 1-6 P.M.
Tasting-room fee: none for estate wines; $5 for four Library Reserve
    Cabernet Sauvignons

Owners: Lillian and Jack Kroustalis
Winemaker: Stephen Rigby
First vines planted: 1972
First year as bonded winery: 1988
First wine release: 1990

Directions: From Winston-Salem, exit Interstate 40 West on to U.S. 421.
After 15 miles on U.S. 421, take Exit 246 (Shallowford Road) and turn left.
Go 2 miles and turn left on Williams Road. The winery is the fourth drive
on the left. From Statesville, take Interstate 40 East to the Farmington
Road exit. Turn left and go 10 miles. Turn right at the second stop sign on
to Courtney-Huntsville Road. Drive 2 miles, then make a hairpin right turn
on to Williams Road. The winery is the fourth drive on the left.

Westbend Vineyards

For Jack and Lillian Kroustalis, a passion for wine has meant committing themselves to a lifelong education. Lillian says of wine, "You live it and learn. When we go to Europe, we visit wineries. In the States, we visit wineries. You're always learning. Wine is not static. There's always something different about it."

They have lived it for over 30 years, but they wouldn't have if they had listened to other people. In the early 1970s, as they considered planting vineyards specializing in European varietals, almost everyone counseled them against it. No one had ever grown French vinifera grapes in the Piedmont. They tried to get advice from state officials, farming experts, and professors at North Carolina State University and the University of North Carolina, but no one could help them. Lillian says, "They just didn't know. They had no experience except with muscadines. The agricultural people said, 'Would you be interested in growing some blueberries?' They wanted us to grow what they knew." The Kroustalises decided to experiment with the grapes anyway, on farmland they had bought near the Yadkin River.

Although Jack and Lillian didn't know it at the time, the land's fertile soil, sloping drainage, and elevation of 950 feet above sea level turned out to be excellent for vineyards. They started on a small scale, planting various varietals including Chardonnay, Cabernet, and Gamay on a few acres at a time. As they traveled the Eastern states to attend viticulture conferences and visit other wineries, they discovered vineyards growing the French-American hybrids Chambourcin and Seyval. Since people continued to insist that their experiment with Chardonnay would fail, Jack and Lillian decided to plant the hybrids as well, as a form of security.

Although the Kroustalises always envisioned a winery as a long-term goal, they developed the vineyards slowly, as they educated themselves. Westbend's basement, which Lillian laughingly refers to as "the Dungeon," still contains wine in unlabeled bottles, leftovers from those early years. For those "vintages," they destemmed the grapes at the kitchen table, crushed them in a pot, and used a manual bottling machine. "We had a lot of fun," Lillian recalls. "We were playing. It was a hobby." They would put a C on the cork to indicate the wine was a Chardonnay and an R to show it was a Riesling. At one point, however, the hobby caused problems. While they were traveling in Europe, an airport x-ray machine outlined some bottles in their baggage. The security guards insisted they unpack and explain the objects. Lillian says, "They wanted to know what it was, and we had to show them. And of course, none of it was labeled. It could have been anything."

By the mid-1980s, the Kroustalises had 30 acres of vines and a 70-ton grape harvest, which they sold to regional wineries. Château Morrisette in Virginia bought much of their crop. When Morrisette's winemaker visited the vineyards and pronounced the grapes excellent, Jack and Lillian knew they were on the right track.

Having successfully grown high-quality grapes, they decided to become more serious about the winemaking itself. They began to convert the farmhouse into a winery, starting with the stable, which was available because, Lillian explains, "my daughter found boys and lost horses." They renovated the space and placed vats where the stalls used to be, but the original double doors can still be seen on tours. They bought professional equipment, became a bonded winery, and hired Steve Shepard as the winemaker in the years 1988 and 1989. As part of the process, they had to decide on a permanent name. It was a difficult choice. They considered and rejected several names, including Yadkin Valley. Lillian recalls, "We didn't want to call it Château something or something French-sounding. And our name, Kroustalis, doesn't flow well on a label." Eventually, they decided to recognize and honor their geographical location. "We are who we are because of where we are," Lillian says. The area around the winery is known as the West Bend region because of a bend to the west of the Yadkin River, and the Kroustalises took that name with only a slight modification—the two words became one.

Westbend had an important early success. Its first vintages, the 1990 Chardonnay and Chambourcin, were awarded several gold medals at the Eastern International Wine Competition. In fact, Westbend was the only winery east of the Mississippi so honored. The medals were particularly impressive because the major California wineries participated in the event, and Westbend's barrel-fermented Chardonnay won in a head-to-head competition against Kendall-Jackson. At the time, wine news didn't garner the media attention it now gets, and the only announcement was a blurb in the local newspaper. However, it did mean immediate credibility for the new winery. Though people at Westbend had considered the wine good, Lillian wryly notes that, "as a mother, you look at your child and you think it's beautiful even when it's homely." The gold medals were crucial outside corroboration.

Westbend quickly gained additional recognition. Some of its 1994 wines were listed as "Best Values" in *Wine Spectator*, and Robert Parker of the *Wine Advocate* called Westbend "one of the South's best kept wine secrets." Praising its Chardonnay, Seyval, Sauvignon,

Lillian and Jack Kroustalis of Westbend Vineyards

and Cabernet Sauvignon, Parker remarked, "As fine as these wines are, I am surprised they are not better known outside of North Carolina." His view of the wines' quality was shared by others through the 1990s, as Westbend's wines continued to win medals at national and international competitions. Because of their stubbornness, hard work, and dedication, the Kroustalises proved that excellent European varietals could be grown in the Piedmont. Larry Ehlers of Chateau Laurinda says, "I think all the wineries in North Carolina have to look back at Westbend with a little bit of gratitude. They did experiments and research on plantings at their own expense, without any outside help, that we all benefit from today. Anybody that makes wine in this state has to recognize that."

Lillian admits, "We had no master plan. . . . We were not in a hurry. We just evolved." Nonetheless, the winery has an integrated, soothing atmosphere. Some visitors come not only to sample the products but also to enjoy the sense of peace the rural setting provides. Many bring picnics, and people frequently linger on the patio. Once, a woman even asked if she could sprinkle her husband's ashes among the vines. Lillian told the distraught widow that she wouldn't give official permission, but she also mentioned when the winery would be deserted. "I don't know if she did it or not," Lillian says. "I never saw her again." Others regard the vineyards as a place for romance. People have come to Westbend on dates, held wedding receptions here, and even made marriage proposals on the property.

Westbend's vines now cover over 75 acres and include more than a dozen varietals. As the grape-growing potential of the Yadkin Valley has become recognized, Lillian and Jack are amused at the number of people who want to grow the crop they were warned against. Yet they welcome the company. They believe that the more quality wineries there are, the better it is for the industry. The competition may also have inspired them. After years of maintaining a status quo, they decided in 1999 that they needed to make major changes. In 2000, they introduced a new label, Shallowford Cellars, and initiated a newsletter, the *Westbend Gazette*. In 2002, the winery's tasting room was moved to a larger space, one framed by wooden beams from a salvaged tobacco warehouse. Westbend has also begun events such as its "Music in the Vineyards."

Ask Lillian why she and Jack have dedicated so much of their lives to wine, and she will respond, "Wine is seductive. It gets you. It grabs you. It won't go away."

Westbend Vineyards Wine List

Whites
Chardonnay, Barrel Fermented Chardonnay, Muscat Cannelli, Riesling, Sauvignon Blanc, Seyval Blanc, Vidal Blanc, Viognier

Rosé
Carolina Blush

Reds

Cabernet Sauvignon, Carolina Cuvée (a blend of Cabernet, Chambourcin, and Merlot), Chambourcin, Merlot

Westbend also offers three table wines under the Shallowford Cellars label—White, Red, and Rosé.

Recipe Suggestions from Westbend Vineyards

Chicken Cacciatore

½ cup olive oil	2 cups tomato, chopped
1 medium onion, chopped	1 tablespoon tomato paste
1 green pepper, chopped	1 cup Westbend Chambourcin
2 cloves garlic, minced	pinch of dry basil
3-pound chicken, cut up, excess fat removed	salt and pepper to taste

Heat olive oil in a large Dutch oven. Add onions, green peppers, and garlic. Add chicken and brown on both sides. Add tomatoes, tomato paste, wine, and seasonings. Cover and cook over low heat for 40 to 45 minutes, turning chicken occasionally and adding wine if more liquid is needed. Cook until chicken is very tender and sauce has cooked down. Serve with a fresh green salad, warm, crusty bread, and the rest of the Chambourcin.

Fondue

Use a Westbend Chardonnay in preparing your favorite savory fondue recipe. Here's a Swiss version.

1 clove garlic, halved
1 cup Westbend Chardonnay or Riesling
1 teaspoon lemon juice
2 cups Gruyère cheese, grated

2 cups Emmental cheese, grated
1 teaspoon corn flour
1 tablespoon kirsch (cherry liqueur)

Rub inside of fondue pot with garlic. Pour in wine and lemon juice and heat gently until bubbling. Reduce heat to low and gradually stir in cheeses. Continue to heat until cheeses melt, stirring frequently. In a small bowl, blend corn flour smoothly with kirsch. Stir corn flour mixture into cheese mixture and cook for 2 to 3 minutes until thick and smooth, stirring frequently. Do not allow fondue to boil. Serve with crusty French bread.

Westbend also recommends using 2 cups of its Seyval Blanc to baste your holiday turkey, basting every 15 minutes during the final hour and a half of roasting.

Westbend Vineyards at Tanglewood

Profile: Dr. Robert McRitchie, Educator and Winemaker, Surry Community College

Dr. Robert McRitchie

To Robert "Bob" McRitchie, the rapid growth of North Carolina's wine industry has a familiar feel. Before joining the viticulture program at Surry Community College, he spent over two decades as a winemaker in Oregon. During that time, the number of Oregon wineries increased from a dozen to over 170, and he suspects a similar expansion could happen in North Carolina.

The key for the state's industry, McRitchie believes, is discovering which varietals will thrive. In Oregon, the Holy Grail was Pinot Noir, which doesn't always do well in the Southeast. Growers need to be patient. Rather than chasing market trends, they need to allow their vineyards' distinct identities to emerge. He tells his students, most of whom are planting vines, "Don't compare this to Napa Valley. This is North Carolina. Furthermore, it's the Piedmont, and it may well be that it will take your lifetime to discover what is the best expression of the place you've located your vineyard."

Although McRitchie has taught in a number of places, the subjects haven't always been viticulture and oenology. A Ph.D. in comparative physiology, he used to teach biology and zoology until a professorship at the University of Wisconsin at Green Bay prompted him to seek a different career. He explains, laughing, "If you've ever lived there, you realize that you want to get away from there in the winter." To escape the Northern cold, he moved his family to the West Coast and found a laboratory job at a Napa Valley winery. Then, after several years in California, he relocated to Oregon, where he became a prominent winemaker.

Twenty years ago, when people asked McRitchie why he left an established wine region for a fledgling one, he responded, "It's a challenge. It's an adventure." He gives the same answer to explain his move to North Carolina. The job at Surry Community College offered a unique opportunity to combine his academic and winemaking careers.

McRitchie enjoys teaching at Surry in part because his classroom is a "fascinating mix." His students include tobacco farmers, bankers, airline pilots, law-enforcement officers, housewives, and high-school students. He notes, "They bring an incredible amount of diversity in thought, opinion, and education into the classroom." Almost all of them have begun vineyards, and many plan to open wineries. He says, "They're actually doing it. That's exciting. They're taking what they're learning in the classroom and putting it to use."

Like all good teachers, McRitchie feels a sense of responsibility to his students. In addition to technical information, he offers general advice. Emphasizing the importance of education and collaboration, he tells them, "Passion is fine—we need it—but reason is an important element as well. You have to be rational. The more you can learn about basic plant science to begin with, and the more you can keep in touch with each other—in what is truly a family—the more you're going to learn and the better off the whole industry is going to be."

McRitchie also believes that people need to guard against losing their perspective and becoming "wine fetishists." He says that a career in the wine industry "is a great adventure. There's no question about it. I don't know anybody professionally that doesn't love the business. But I think it can devour you. I've seen it happen. I've seen people so consumed by what they're doing that they lose wife and family and sometimes land and money. I always tell my students to maintain a balance in their life. It's just as important in your life as it is in that bottle of wine you're trying to make."

Wineries of Eastern North Carolina

Bennett Vineyards
Duplin Wine Cellars
Martin Vineyards
Moonrise Bay Vineyard
Silver Coast Winery

Bennett Vineyards

P.O. Box 150
6832 Bonnerton Road
Edward, N.C. 27821
Phone: 877-762-9463 or 252-322-7154
Fax: 252-946-5965
Website: www.ncwines.com
E-mail: bud157jr@inetww.com or ncwine@newbernnc.net
Hours: Monday-Saturday, 2-5 P.M.; please call ahead

Owners: Buddy Harrell and Robert Thornton
Winemaker: Buddy Harrell, Jr.
First vines planted: 1991
First year as bonded winery: 1993
First wine release: 1993

Directions: From Greenville, take N.C. 33 East to S.R. 1936
and turn right. Drive approximately 0.5 mile, turn right on
Bennett Vineyards Road (formerly Old Sand Hill Road), and
go approximately 1 mile. The winery is on the right.

Some people consider the wine business romantic, but Buddy Harrell
isn't one of them. He knows too much about what can go wrong.
In the decade since he co-founded Bennett Vineyards, he has en-
dured several hurricanes, a devastating frost, the death of a partner,
near-bankruptcies, and other misfortunes. Nevertheless, he has per-

Buddy Harrell, Jr., Bennett Vineyards

sisted in trying to make the vineyards productive.

In 1990, Robert Godley approached Buddy with an idea. He had family property that he thought would be good for growing grapes, and he knew that Buddy had an old family recipe from his grandfather for making muscadine wine. He suggested they put these two assets together. The men agreed to become partners and formed Bennett Vineyards. The next year, they began planting vines.

Although at first the venture seemed solid, two hurricanes in 1996 damaged much of the vineyards. That same year, Robert died, and Buddy discovered that the title to the land was a tangled matter. As a result, he found himself ineligible for disaster relief funds and unable to borrow money from banks. Finally, in 1998, after twice considering bankruptcy, he decided to take a calculated risk. He let the bank foreclose on the property, then, when the vineyards were sold at public auction, he bought them back. He then had a clear title, but his troubles didn't end. More hurricanes struck, flooding the land, destroying trellis systems, and damaging vines. In 2001, an April freeze ruined 50 to 60 percent of the crop. Having grown tired of the constant struggles, and realizing that he didn't have enough time to devote to the vineyards, Buddy turned its management over to his son Buddy Harrell, Jr.

Although he doesn't have an agricultural or viticultural background, Buddy Jr. insists that "it's not hard to grow things. You just have to find a little bit about what they're about." In his first two years, Buddy Jr. devoted himself to "trying to reorganize and restructure and make the place look good." He admits, "The wine was getting out of shape. The grass was taller than the vines." He restacked hundreds of broken poles left from the hurricanes, moved scattered piles of railroad ties, and regraded the winery's entrance. A former cook, he knows the importance of presentation. He says, "When they see the plate, that's the first impression." Consequently, he has paid particular attention to the front of the property because "if that looks good, then everything else will look good."

Bennett Vineyards has some you-pick grapes available, but for the most part, it has concentrated on selling its wines at farmers' markets and festivals, rather than catering to visitors. For example, although the winery posts regular hours, people are urged to call ahead because, Buddy Jr. admits, "sometimes I just close up and go." Tours can be scheduled, but people who expect to see the standard barrel room, fermentation room, and stainless-steel tanks will be disappointed. Bennett Vineyards takes a more basic approach. The winery operates in a small building with minimal equipment. At the moment, there is no indoor tasting room. Instead, a covered outdoor area with metal patio tables provides a place to try wines.

In its promotional materials, Bennett Vineyards emphasizes the history of winemaking in the United States and the South. Because muscadine is a native grape, one noted by the first European explorers and settlers, Bennett Vineyards calls itself the "Vintners of America's First Wine." A brochure claims the wines give "a true taste of our American colonial experience." To emphasize this connection, Bennett's wines have been named after colonial places—for example, Williamsburg White, Mount Vernon White, and Jamestown Red.

The name of the winery also reflects a claim to a heritage. Robert Godley believed that at one time, the land was owned by the Bennetts, one of the area's oldest families. Grapes were even grown here in the 19th century, when the property was part of the Wiley T. Bennett plantation. Behind part of the vineyards is a small graveyard where, Buddy Jr. says, many members of the Bennett family are buried.

In the future, Bennett Vineyards hopes to attract more visitors. Buddy Sr. and his wife, Helen, are building a bed-and-breakfast on the property, and Buddy Jr. has considered putting fish ponds among the vineyards as points of interest. For now, however, Buddy Jr. plans to concentrate on improving the business's appearance and learning how to improve the wines themselves. He has put in a line for county water in order to have a consistent, clean water supply, and he has begun to experiment with blending to change the color of the wines. He admits, "I'm still kind of learning." Although it's doubtful the hurricanes will stop coming, Buddy Jr. is optimistic about the future. He insists of the winery, "You can make money with it. You just got to know how to do it."

Bennett Vineyards Wine List

 ### Whites
Mount Vernon White, Williamsburg White

 ### Rosé
Plymouth Blush

 ### Reds
Charlestown Red, Jamestown Red, Roanoke Red

 ### Fruit wines (limited availability)
Strawberry, Watermelon

CAROLINA
HATTERAS RED
SWEET MUSCADINE WINE
Alcohol 12% by Volume

$\mathcal{D}$uplin Wine Cellars

P.O. Box 756
Rose Hill, N.C. 28458
Phone: 800-774-9634 or 910-289-3888
Fax: 910-289-3094
Website: www.duplinwinery.com
On-line ordering available
E-mail: duplinwinery@hotmail.com
Hours: Monday-Thursday, 9 A.M.-6 P.M.; Friday, 9 A.M.-9 P.M.;
    Saturday, 9 A.M.-6 P.M.
Tasting-room fee: none

Owners: David Fussell and family
Winemakers: David Fussell and family
First vines planted: 1972
First year as bonded winery: 1976
First wine release: 1976

Directions: Take Exit 380 off Interstate 40 and follow the road

In 1995, after two decades of being in business, Duplin Wine Cellars had its first profitable year. David Fussell, a co-owner and co-founder, credits the Danes. In the mid-1990s, researchers published the "Copenhagen City Heart Study," which showed that the mortality risk for those who drink moderate amounts of wine is lower

David Fussell

than for those who drink other spirits or are teetotalers. In short, the study said that wine drinkers tend to live longer than other people. Additional studies have suggested that this may be because some wines contain antioxidants. Muscadine grapes, in particular, have high levels. This fact, David says, got Duplin Wine Cellars "out of the red and into the black." Sales took off when *60 Minutes* featured the Copenhagen study in a news report. Now, people write from as far away as China requesting Duplin products. David is excited but cautious about the winery's prospects. He insists, "Man can make his plans, but the final outcome is up to the Lord. The pendulum can swing right back." He speaks from experience. He and Duplin Wine Cellars have already gone through dramatic ups and downs.

David traces the winery's origins to the 1960s, when the Department of Agriculture was promoting grapes as a "wonder crop" and Canandaigua Wines was paying farmers $350 a ton for muscadines. After attending an information meeting sponsored by the state, David's brother, Dan, suggested they try to grow grapes. So, in 1972, in addition to raising hogs and planting tobacco, corn, and sweet potatoes, the brothers put in 10 acres of Carlos vines. Later that year, the crop's price plummeted to $150 a ton. The area's farmers met to discuss what could be done with their 2,492 acres of grapes, and David and Dan decided to see if opening a winery was a feasible option. They visited two small regional wineries and worked out the cost projections with one of the owners. David recalls, "It was going to cost $76,000, and on the way home I can remember talking with my brother, and we said, 'Ain't no way. Ain't no way in the world we're going to spend that much money to build a winery.' And that's true, we didn't. We spent a whole lot more."

Eventually, the Fussells founded Duplin Wine Cellars, the 26th winery in the state to be bonded since Prohibition. To raise money, they sold stock to 14 local farmers. In the beginning, David explains with a laugh, they needed to figure out how to make wine, since they were "Southern boys" and "wine was not the official drink of the South in the 70s." They read every book they could find, talked to experts at North Carolina State University, and made 30 different test batches in five-gallon carboys. Once they decided on a recipe, they made 3,000 gallons in 1976 for Duplin's first commercial release. At the time, because they had no specialized equipment, they moved the juice in buckets, unloaded the grapes with a front-end loader on a tractor, and crushed them using equipment that Dan built. David remembers when he delivered the winery's first order to Raleigh: "We were still in the hog trade, so I got my water hose and cleaned my hog trailer up real good. Got all the manure out of it and put our wine in the hog trailer to carry it to one of these sophisticated distributorships in Raleigh." When he got to the company, everyone came out, shaking their heads. Someone said, "We've seen a lot, but this is the first time that we've seen anybody bring us wine on a hog trailer."

Duplin Winery

In the next 10 years, Duplin Wine Cellars grew rapidly. It sold everything it could make. By 1983, it was producing 200,000 gallons of wine. The rest of the decade, however, was disastrous for the business. Changes in tax laws and new legislation regarding distribution resulted in plummeting sales. Then, according to David, a bad investment in the (now bankrupt) Southland Estate Winery "almost pulled us under." He insists, "I really did not think we would survive." The banks took everything but the winery itself. David had to sell off all the large tanks and "any nice equipment that we could get any money for" so that he could meet payroll and buy grapes. He lost his house and had to get a full-time teaching job. He admits that during those years, he often thought about quitting, but his wife, Ann, would say, "We've invested this much time and effort in it; let's try one more day. Don't throw in the towel today." David notes, "She was actually stronger than me. She was the one that kept it going during those hard times." While he taught, Ann ran the winery.

The Fussells' resilience and commitment sustained Duplin Wine Cellars until, as David puts it, "the health issue turned us around." Now, sales again seem ready to reach impressive levels, and the winery is expanding dramatically. Although much of this growth stems from the positive press generated by medical research, Duplin also has achieved recognition because of its success at competitions. For example, at the 2002 San Diego National Wine Competition, its Pink Magnolia received a double gold medal and was voted the "Best of Class." All of this makes David optimistic about muscadines, which he believes "have as good a future, if not better, than any other agricultural crop in the state."

Not surprisingly, a visit to Duplin Wine Cellars is partly an educational seminar on the health benefits of wine. In the tasting room, handouts contain quotations from doctors around the world, and winery staff claim that over 500 studies have findings similar to the Copenhagen one. Suggesting that "if you want to age more gracefully, you'll start taking in natural antioxidants," David points out that "wine is the highest natural product in antioxidants that the Lord has chosen to make." He says, "It's not a cure-all, but it's like a seat belt. If you're in a wreck, you might die, but that seat belt might cut your risks." The winery regularly receives letters testifying to its wines' positive effects on a range of problems including high cholesterol, arthritis, heart disease, obesity, and cancer. In fact, in the future, David foresees "a big muscadine industry in the state, with more of it going into health products than is going into wine." Already, Duplin offers some "nutraceutical" products. These include pills consisting of crushed grape seeds, which contain high amounts of antioxidants, and a nonalcoholic tonic called Resveratrol.

In addition to its muscadine wines and products, Duplin Wine Cellars has an extensive wine list that includes vinifera wines such as Chardonnay, Merlot, and Cabernet Sauvignon, fruit wines, alcohol-free wines, sparkling wines, port, and sherry. Many of these can be tried in the winery's large tasting room. Duplin also has a gift shop that includes a selection of wine-related products, a jewelry counter, a glassware section, gourmet food items, and a tasting bar devoted to jams, jellies, and salad dressings.

Since, as David notes, "Rose Hill is not a tourist mecca," the winery offers monthly dinner shows featuring different musical acts. In 2001, Duplin opened The Bistro, which serves lunch and dinner. The winery's theater and dining facilities can be rented for group events. Both of these spaces contain interesting historical items from the state's 200-year-old wine industry. These include old Duplin bottles, advertisements and bottles from other North Carolina wineries, and antique equipment.

The oldest winery in North Carolina, Duplin also has some of the strongest local roots. It still buys grapes from 12 of the original stock-holding farmers, and it has another 10 farmers in the area under contract. One of the larger employers in the town, Duplin has a payroll of over 20 people, most of whom are named Fussell. In part, this is because the winery is very much a family enterprise. David's brother, wife, father, sons, daughters-in-law, etc., all work there. However, it is also true that almost every business in southern Duplin County employs Fussells, since over 50 families by that name live in the area. Each can trace its lineage back to Benjamin Fussell, David's great-grandfather, who moved to Rose Hill from England in 1732. For example, The Bistro's chef, William Fussell, is descended from one of Benjamin Fussell's sons, while David is descended from another.

Besides its deep Southern roots, David's family has strong religious beliefs. In both the gift shop and the meeting room at Duplin Wine Cellars, large wooden signs announce, "To God Be the Glory." The bathrooms display the Apostles' Creed. Discussions about alcohol consumption are put in religious terms. One Fussell points out, "The Lord advises everything has to be in moderation." Another family member explains that the Lord has put a natural regulator in your body, so "as soon as you begin to feel the alcohol, you should quit drinking." In fact, the Fussells believe that God has taken a hand in their business. David says, "I feel real good about what God is doing here in the health industry, because we're not doing it. It's a gift."

Because of his religious beliefs, going into the wine business was not an easy decision for David. In addition to financial and agricultural concerns, he had to consider spiritual ones. Although numerous passages in the Bible discuss wine in a positive way, many people of David's faith insist on complete abstinence from alcohol. So before committing to the winery, David prayed. He says that, as he asked the Lord for guidance, "a vision came to go ahead and do this because what [we're] doing is going to help people. Now, that was beyond my comprehension. I said, 'Lord, what do you mean it's going to help people?' And he never revealed that to me." For David, then, the winery is a type of divine mission. He feels that it offers people products that God has put in nature for their benefit. Reflecting on his prayer, David says, "I didn't understand at that time, and I still don't understand the full ramifications of the vision, but I'm beginning to. Now, I can sort of see with this health issue what he had in mind. And I really think we're going to help people."

Duplin Wine Cellars Wine List

Vinifera Whites
Carolina Mist, Chardonnay

Vinifera Reds
Cabernet Sauvignon, Merlot

Muscadine Whites
Carlos, Magnolia, Scuppernong

Muscadine Reds
Burgundy, Carolina Red, Hatteras Red, Pink Magnolia

Rosé
Scuppernong Blush

Fruit wine
Blackberry

Duplin also offers ports, sherries, sparkling wines, alcohol-free wines, and "nutraceuticals."

Recipe Suggestions from Duplin Wine Cellars

Carlos with Shrimp

12 medium shrimp	1 clove garlic, minced
2 tablespoons butter	½ cup Duplin Wine Cellars Carlos
juice of 1 lemon	

Sauté shrimp in butter, lemon juice, and garlic until just pink. Add Carlos and simmer for 5 to 10 minutes until liquid is reduced by half. Serves 4 as an appetizer.

Magnolia with Chicken Breasts

4 chicken breast halves	2 tablespoons olive oil
1 cup Duplin Wine Cellars Magnolia	2 tablespoons butter
½ cup Italian dressing	4 tablespoons muscadine jelly

Marinate chicken in wine and Italian dressing, then sauté in olive oil and butter until golden brown and cooked thoroughly. Spread 1 tablespoon jelly on each chicken breast. Serve with wild rice. Serves 4.

Profile: Tania Dautlick, Executive Director, North Carolina Grape Council

When Tania Dautlick interviewed for her job with the North Carolina Grape Council, she was asked if she drank wine. It was an unofficial but important requirement for someone who would be responsible for helping to develop the state's grape industry. Luckily, she could say yes, although she admits that, "at 25, I hadn't been drinking wine seriously for a long time." Thanks to her B.A. in plant science and M.A. in horticulture, she felt confident about the agricultural aspects of the job, but she immediately enrolled in a wine-tasting class and set out to learn more about viticulture.

Established in 1986 and housed in the North Carolina Department of Agriculture, the Grape Council promotes the development of the grape and wine industries through research, education, and marketing. Consequently, Dautlick finds herself doing a wide variety of tasks. One day, she might be working with researchers at North Carolina State University and Surry Community College, while the next, she might be reviewing ad campaigns. Dautlick says, "It's been an ideal job for me because it's so diverse." The one constant has been the inquiries. She gets daily calls from consumers, journalists, state legislators, growers, people thinking about starting wineries, and people who want to know the location of you-pick muscadine vineyards. In short, almost anyone with a question about North Carolina grapes and wine contacts Dautlick's office.

Because the Grape Council acts as a clearinghouse for information, Dautlick's name is one of the most widely known in the industry. It also is one of the most respected. Winery and vineyard owners praise her enthusiasm and help. "She has done a magnificent job of promoting and finally getting interest cranked up in the state," Bob Howard of The Teensy Winery says. "Without her, we would still be in the doldrums." The admiration is mutual. Dautlick insists the best part of her job "is definitely all the people that I get to meet. The people who are involved in the field are so interesting and diverse. They're mostly strong personalities." She has developed an enormous respect for those who work with grapes because "it's a lifestyle commitment. It's all-consuming, which is the case with many small businesses. But this one in particular, you have to be on call 24 hours a day for your plants and your wines and your customers."

Dautlick has seen the industry grow dramatically. When she began working for the Grape Council in 1995, there were 68 vineyards and a handful of wineries

Tania Dautlick

in North Carolina. Now, there are more than 240 vineyards and almost two dozen wineries. In fact, in October 2001, Dautlick's office organized North Carolina's first commercial wine competition. Six judges tasted more than 75 entries from 14 wineries. Dautlick considers it one of the highlights of her career: "I was so proud to be watching them tasting the wines blind and to see their reaction and to learn how impressed they were and how high they scored the wine." She says with satisfaction, "It just made me feel really proud of how far we've come."

 *artin Vineyards*

P.O. Box 186
Knotts Island, N.C. 27950
Phone: 252-429-3542 or 252-429-3564
Fax: 252-429-3095
Website: www.martinvineyards.com
On-line ordering available
E-mail: Lulu1926@aol.com
Hours: Monday-Saturday, 10 A.M.-6 P.M.; Sunday, noon-6 P.M.;
    closed in late winter
Tasting-room fee: $5 for five wines and a souvenir glass; fee is
    refunded with the purchase of a bottle.

Owners: David and Jeannie Martin
Winemaker: David Martin
First vines planted: 1987
First year as bonded winery: 1993
First wine release: 1993

Directions: From Virginia Beach, Virginia, take Princess Anne
Road south to Knotts Island, just across the North Carolina
border. Bear left at the Knotts Island Market and go approxi-
mately 1 mile to the vineyards, located on the left. From
Currituck County, take N.C. 168 to the free Currituck Sound ferry
(call 800-BY FERRY for information). After crossing the sound to
Knotts Island, follow N.C. 615 North for 2.7 miles to Martin Farm
Lane. The entrance to the winery is on the right.

David Martin

David Martin's career as a farmer began early. Almost as soon as he could walk, he started helping his father, William Martin, on the family's strawberry farm in Virginia Beach. He loved working in the dirt and playing with plants, and when he wandered away from the fields, it wasn't to watch television, but to go into the woods. He says, "I like to watch things grow. I've always been a plant person." Unlike his brothers, who moved away to pursue teaching and coaching careers, David returned home after college to plant the family orchards. He has remained there ever since.

It's hardly surprising that David knows the 88 acres of Martin Vineyards intimately, since he helped plant the trees and vines as a 22-year-old. In the early 1970s, his father decided to move the family from Virginia Beach to Knotts Island. He bought a cattle farm that was slated to become a housing development, but instead of putting buildings on the property, he planted fruit trees. It was an appropriate place for an orchard. Knotts Island has a history of fruit farming that dates to the 1800s; the township is even called "Fruitville." In addition to apples and peaches, the Martins planted strawberries and scuppernong vines. Their you-pick crops attracted a loyal clientele. David says, "People came back every year like clockwork."

In 1987, looking for new agricultural challenges, David decided to experiment with vinifera varietals. He planted several rows of vines and began teaching himself how to make wine. At first, he worked with an old manual press that can still be seen on the winery's porch. He says, "I took a hands-on approach. I learned from the ground up, which is a good way to do it." He is self-taught. In fact, if he had listened to advice, the vineyards wouldn't exist. People at North Carolina State University and Virginia Tech warned him that he wouldn't be able to grow vinifera successfully because it would develop Pierce's disease, which often infects grapevines in mild climates. Although David acknowledges that some of the crop has been affected, he believes he has found ways to combat the disease.

In 1992, David planted more vines, but he soon discovered that he "had too much wine. I couldn't drink it all or give it all away, so we said, 'Well, let's get a wine permit.' " Martin Vineyards became a bonded winery and now has eight acres dedicated to vinifera varietals. Although David says that "we specialize in the Bordeaux reds: Cabernet, Merlot, Cabernet Franc, Petit Verdot, and Malbec," he also makes muscadine and fruit wines that sell out quickly each year. In fact, they are so popular that people reserve bottles months in advance. Jeannie Martin calls the muscadine wine "liquid gold." She says, "I could have thousands of recordings of people saying, 'Oh, my God, it tastes just like the grapes at my grandmother's house.' It's the state taste."

Because making a good wine takes good grapes, David believes that "most of the work is in the fields. If you don't do the work out there, what's done in the winery means nothing." Overall, he calculates that each grape cluster is worked on at least four times in the course of a season, an estimate that doesn't include tucking the vines and trimming them. Then, when it comes time to harvest, a grower needs to know not only when to pick, but how. David explains, "You've got to get the grapes ripe, and uniformly ripe. That means saving only the shoots that are uniform and saving the best clusters. If you go in and pick them all the same day, you're going to have bunches that are ripe, overripe, and underripe." Consequently, he picks three times a year. Insisting that "there's no short cuts," he points out that "it's total work out here. Seven days a week. You've got to love it, or it will drive you absolutely bonkers." He also notes, "You've got to have a good wife. An understanding wife. You're working here until dark."

According to David, experts who say the coast is a bad place to farm fail to take into account Knotts Island's unique climate. The area is an excellent place for fruit because, he explains, "we don't get a lot of the rainfall that they get just inland from here. The ocean breezes knock it back." The breezes also quickly dry any moisture that does occur, which keeps rot at a minimum. The island's sandy soil provides excellent drainage. David says vines "root like crazy here. Stick a vine cutting in the ground, come back the next year, and it's growing." In fact, the vines can be too vigorous. He constantly needs to cut them back to ensure a quality yield. Even the coast's periodic hurricanes don't damage the vines. They do, however, make for difficult working conditions. David remembers when he was harvesting his Merlot in 1998: "I picked it two days before Hurricane Bonnie. I actually had it out here fermenting. I built walls around it and wrapped it in tarps, in case it got really bad, which it did. Trees were down all over. Right on the coast here, we really take the hit." In spite of Bonnie, the Merlot turned out to be "a great wine."

Because it ripens early, before hurricane season, Merlot usually does well. David also likes his Viognier, which "has turned out to be real nice." He points out, "We had the first Viognier on the market in the state. Now, you see it all over." David has had to experiment to determine what grows best: "When I started here, it was unknown what would do well. It had never been done here." The closest winery was in Williamsburg, Virginia. Now, other people have begun to develop vineyards in the area. For example, David helped nearby Moonrise Bay Vineyard get started by selling it its first cuttings. He laughs, "We've got a little wine appellation growing here. It helps, having the two wineries."

To attract visitors, Martin Vineyards has you-pick orchards and has begun to host events on major holidays such as Memorial Day and the Fourth of July. The entrance to the property is beautiful. A dirt road bordered by white fences goes through the orchards and vineyards and past the Martin family's 19th-century residence. The winery itself, however, is a working farm, rather than a showcase for visitors. The small tasting room has examples of work by local artists, but most people will probably want to stay outside, where tables at the water's edge allow them to picnic, look at the bay, or bird-watch. The fruit trees attract so many ospreys and other birds that Jeannie says the orchards can be "like an airport." In fact, when David designed the winery's labels, he included an osprey.

In addition to being hand-bottled, Martin Vineyards wines are hand-labeled. Jeannie does this in her spare time in the tasting room. Each year, she has more work to do because the winery is steadily increasing production.

Martin Vineyards' success has a clear cause; it's the effort that David exerts in the fields. He does it because "I love farming. I love producing a good crop. It's hard to do, but when you see the people come out and pick, and taste the wine, that's rewarding."

Martin Vineyards Wine List

 ### Whites
Chardonnay, Fruitville White, Muscadine, Viognier

 ### Reds
Atlantis Meritage, Cabernet Sauvignon, Merlot

 ### Fruit wines
Bay Orchard Apple, Strawberry, Peach

Recipe Suggestions from Martin Vineyards

Muscadine Cake

Cake

1 box white cake mix   Martin Vineyards Muscadine Wine

Glaze

½ cup Martin Vineyards Muscadine Wine   ¼ cup confectioners' sugar

Prepare cake according to package directions, substituting Martin Vineyards Muscadine for water.

To prepare glaze, bring ½ cup Martin Vineyards Muscadine and confectioners' sugar to a boil.

Glaze top of cake and serve.

Summertime Delight

1 bottle Martin Vineyards Peach Wine   1 bottle Martin Vineyards Muscadine Wine

Mix wines and serve.

Strawberry Mimosas

1 bottle Martin Vineyards Strawberry Wine   1 bottle champagne

Mix wine with champagne and serve.

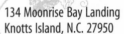Moonrise Bay Vineyard

134 Moonrise Bay Landing
Knotts Island, N.C. 27950
Phone: 866-888-9463 or 252-429-9463
Fax: 252-429-3090
Website: www.moonrisebaywine.com
E-mail: okmorris@earthlink.net
Hours: Thursday-Sunday, noon-6 P.M.; other times by appointment
Tasting-room fee: none

Owners: Kate Morris, Richard Morris, and Fleet Smith
Winemaker: Richard Morris
First vines planted: 1997
First year as bonded winery: 2000
First wine release: 2001

Directions: From Virginia Beach, Virginia, take Princess Anne Road
south to Knotts Island, just across the North Carolina border. Bear
left at the Knotts Island Market and go 1 mile. The vineyard is on the
left. From Currituck County, take N.C. 168 to the free Currituck
Sound ferry (call 800-BY FERRY for information). After crossing the
sound to Knotts Island, follow N.C. 615 North for 2.8 miles. The
winery entrance is on the right.

Moonrise Bay Vineyard had its origin in a walk in San Francisco.
That's when Richard "Oakie" Morris, a plastic surgeon with a 20-
year practice in Virginia Beach, turned to his longtime office manager and said, "Kate, I don't want to complicate your life, but I love

Moonrise Bay Vineyard Tasting Room

Kate and Richard Morris

you." Unsure what to say, Kate turned away and asked, "What kind of flowers are those?" "They're cyclamens," Oakie answered. Kate laughs at the memory of that morning: "I thought, 'Surely, he's lost his mind.' " Later, after she was convinced of his seriousness and they, as Oakie puts it, "sorted things out and got our lives in order," the couple bought a house on Knotts Island. They had no intention of starting a winery; they were "just thinking of a place to live away from the world," Oakie says.

Their first year on the island, the Morrises found themselves with an unexpected problem: too many pears. Their tree had produced a bumper crop, and even though Kate loves to cook, bushels of pears still remained after she made pear bread, pear pastries, pear desserts, and other pear products. One day, she came home to discover that Oakie had started fermenting pears in a tub. He had decided to make pear wine. Kate remembers that, during the process, "there were flies everywhere. It was a mess. We had two of us straining it though cheesecloth and pressing it." The couple put the five-gallon batch in unlabeled bottles. As an experiment, they served the wine at a Christmas party. When the guests raved about it, insisting it was the best Chardonnay they'd ever tasted, the Morrises' careers as winemakers began.

Encouraged by the response to their pear wine, and having

noticed how well grapes grew at nearby Martin Vineyards, Kate and Oakie decided to plant some vines as a hobby. They bought 1,500 cuttings of Merlot and Cabernet varietals from David Martin. Oakie admits, "I was just going to make a little home-brew. I had no clue how many grapes you'd get off that." He had made "home-brew" before. While studying for his M.D., he often made beer. Although it was popular, Oakie insists that this was no indication of quality because "medical students will drink anything." After his internship, Oakie was drafted. For a while, even in the service, he continued his hobby. He fermented batches in a barracks bathtub. He remembers, "When the commanding officer came by, we put up a sign that said the plumbing was out of order. That explained the *bloup bloup bloup* sound." Eventually, Oakie was stationed in Germany, where the local beers were so good and inexpensive there was no reason to make his own. While in Europe, he also "fell in love with wine." Because he was posted only five kilometers from France, he often crossed the border to eat and to drink "the wonderful French table wines."

As Oakie grew his first grapes on Knotts Island and planned his retirement, he devoted himself to learning about viticulture and oenology. Kate says that he read "for three years at night in his study. I knew we were in trouble because when he makes his mind up to do something, he is going to do it." He toured vineyards, talked to experts in the state's wine industry, and took courses and seminars at the University of California at Davis. Eventually, the Morrises made the commitment to a full-scale commercial vineyard.

Even with Okie's research and drive, it was difficult to establish Moonrise Bay Vineyard. Kate remembers, "The first year was hard. I hated it. Oakie was working 14- to 18-hour days and coming home and falling asleep in his soup. . . . Sometimes, it felt like I had died and it wasn't heaven I woke up in." The following years were also stressful, as the vines grew and needed to be trellised. Kate acknowledges, however, that there were also moments of beauty. When harvesting the Sauvignon Blanc, she remembers how the juice ran down her hands, attracting monarchs and swallow-tails: "You would pick the grapes, and your arms would be full of butterflies. It was beautiful."

As the vineyard matured, the Morrises discovered that Knotts Island has special agricultural properties. According to Oakie, "if you ask the experts, they say you can't grow grapes here. It's too hot and too much disease pressure." However, because of its geography, the island has its own climate. In the summer, it is 10 degrees cooler than places inland, and the constant breezes keep the vines dry and reduce moisture-related problems. Even a heavy dew or rain will quickly evaporate. The tides are wind-driven, and since the nearest opening to the ocean is 50 miles away, the area isn't susceptible to flooding. Hurricanes, the coastal region's main concern, usually arrive too late in the growing season to significantly damage the vines. Consequently, grapes and other fruit crops do very well on the island.

To protect the winery from hurricanes, the Morrises decided to use a Quonset hut that can withstand 180-mile-per-hour winds. Oakie admits, "It looks funny on the outside, but it's nice on the inside." Although the building isn't picturesque, the location is. When the nighttime weather permits, you can watch the moon rise over the bay, a view that inspired both the winery's name and Okie's design for the label. In fact, Moonrise Bay Vineyard sometimes schedules special tastings to coincide with full moons and the lunar calendar. It also hosts events such as candlelight barrel tastings for Valentine's Day, a Fourth of July barbecue, and harvest parties.

In addition to organizing events for large groups, the Morrises occasionally offer wine dinners for a dozen people. These begin at the winery with hors d'oeuvres and barrel tastings. After an hour or so, everyone moves to the Morrises' nearby home for a multicourse candlelight meal with matching Moonrise Bay wines. The house is tucked into a grove of trees at the water's edge. Originally a hunting and fishing club built in 1884, the building was in a "disgusting state" when Kate and Oakie bought it. By stripping away decades of grime, restoring the wood floors, and renovating each room, the

Morrises have made it into a stunning living space, one that provides a wonderful atmosphere for entertaining. Winery dinners have a personal feel because guests not only are invited into the Morrises' home, but Kate and her sister do all the cooking, and Kate's children serve as the wait staff.

The winery itself is, Oakie points out, "a family operation." The children help in the vineyard, the tasting room, and the barrel room. Kate says proudly, "They know what needs to be done, and they do it." Although the children were initially skeptical about the business—one daughter admits that she thought her mother and Oakie "were crazy" and "wouldn't go through with it"—they now think having a winery is "kind of cool work." Other family members who contribute are Kate's mother, who regularly comes from Virginia Beach to assist in the tasting room, and Kate's brother-in-law, Arthur Trottier, who has taken over the management of the vineyard. Calling Arthur "Oakie's right hand," Kate says, "He truly nurtures the vineyard. He spends many sleepless nights when the weather conditions as well as other factors are affecting the grapes." In the future, there will be plenty of additional work for family members who want to help because the Morrises plan to establish another vineyard across the border in Virginia. This will be called "Kate's Vineyard," and the grapes may be used for sparkling wines.

Although the Morrises have worked hard to establish Moonrise Bay Vineyard, they remain on guard against growing too big. They don't want to get to the point where, in Oakie's words, "it becomes a real commercial enterprise, rather than an art form." He explains, "I don't want to be a person in a corporate office. That's not why I got into this." For Oakie, "making wine is a very soulful thing." He values the artistic and aesthetic aspects of the process. For example, he particularly enjoys using tubs instead of tanks because "it's very personal. You taste it. You work with it."

An attempt to find a place away from the world unexpectedly turned the Morrises into winemakers. It's a transformation they appreciate. Kate says, "Sometimes, we're walking in the vineyard in the evening, and it's like a dream. I'm so grateful that we're getting to enjoy it. It's so peaceful." As for Oakie, he admits, "I just love the whole process. Just being involved with it from planting to harvesting, it's all such a neat experience."

𝓜oonrise Bay Vineyard Wine List

Whites
Chardonnay, Sauvignon Blanc

Reds
Cabernet Sauvignon, Chambourcin, Merlot, Norton, Sangiovese, Syrah

Fruit wines
Blackberry, Blueberry, Pear, Raspberry, Strawberry

𝓡ecipe Suggestion from Moonrise Bay Vineyard

𝓜oonrise Bay Vineyard Sangria

2 bottles Moonrise Bay Chambourcin	¹/₃ cup Grand Marnier
1 quart strawberries, sliced	¹/₄ to ¹/₃ cup sugar
1 cup apple juice	1 cinnamon stick

Combine all ingredients in a large pitcher. Stir until sugar dissolves. Cover and refrigerate for 4 hours. Remove cinnamon stick before pouring into glasses to serve.

Silver Coast Winery

6608 Barbeque Road
Ocean Isle Beach, N.C. 28470
Phone: 910-287-2800
Fax: 910-457-0608
Website: www.silvercoastwinery.com
E-mail: info@silvercoastwinery.com
Hours: Monday-Saturday, 11 A.M.-6 P.M., and Sunday, noon-5 P.M.;
    winter hours (November-March), Thursday-Saturday,
    11 A.M.-6 P.M., and Sunday, noon-5 P.M.
Tasting-room fee: none

Owners: Maryann and John Azzato
First vines planted: 2002
First year as bonded winery: 2002
First wine release: 2002

Directions: Take U.S. 17 to N.C. 904. Drive 2 miles west on N.C. 904
to Russtown Road, turn right, go 1.5 miles to Barbeque Road, and
turn right again. The winery is at the end of the road.

On May 17, 2002, as Maryann Azzato's oldest daughter watched a crowd of people tasting wine, looking at art, and listening to music, she leaned over and said, "I'm proud of you, Mom." She had reason to be. In a short period of time, her mother had conceptualized, built, and opened an impressive winery.

Maryann Azzato

Maryann's achievement in establishing Silver Coast Winery is even more notable since she is new to the industry. In the 1990s, she worked as a trader in the financial markets, but she wanted to find a different career because, she says, "the market scared me" and because she didn't enjoy trading. She believes that "in order to have a fulfilling life, you have to like your work. If you don't like your work, there's no point; you've got to find another job."

At first, Maryann considered a mail-order wine business. She had been interested in wine for a long time. Her father made a batch every year with friends, which, she says, "was something that was always fascinating to me." She also collected bottles and labels. After researching the idea, however, she decided it wasn't feasible. Then, as she considered other possibilities, she received one of those phone calls that changes a person's life. A friend told her about a Massachusetts winery that was selling its assets. Suddenly, Maryann had a chance to buy equipment with which she could open a winery. After the call, "my husband looked at me, and I looked at him," she says. They knew it was an enormous commitment, and they decided to make it.

Although Maryann says she never hesitates to "take a little bit of a gamble," she also does her research. After analyzing the region's demographics, the Azzatos bought property near Ocean Isle Beach. This meant Maryann would have to commute 45 minutes from their home, but it placed the winery within a hundred-mile radius of 15 million annual visitors. Besides attracting people from Wilmington, Silver Coast Winery would have the potential to draw visitors from Myrtle Beach and other parts of South Carolina.

The winery's grand opening was the first of many parties. Silver Coast hosts monthly events including the Purple Feet Harvest Festival and an Octoberfest. Its large back patio, designed for groups, has picnic and bistro tables, sun umbrellas, a horseshoe pit, and a stage. In fact, the property has a tradition of good times. For years, it was the site of a "barbecue barn" where people ate and danced. Almost every day, visitors to Silver Coast's tasting room say, "We used to come in when it was Sim's Barbecue." They reminisce about the pickers who played and the clogging they did. Although Maryann wanted to preserve parts of the old building, the wood was too decayed. She did manage to keep the barn's stone fireplace, which now anchors what she calls the winery's "winter room."

The winery's other areas include a tasting bar, a country-store gift shop, and an enormous barrel room inspired by the cave at Shelton Vineyards. Maryann says, "When I was working on the design of the barrel room, I told my husband that I was going to put a waterfall in, and he told me, 'Maryann, if you're going to put a waterfall, *put a waterfall.*' " She took his advice. The waterfall takes up one wall and creates, she believes, "a wonderful soothing feeling." When the winery opened, people immediately asked to book the room for parties, wedding receptions, and meetings. As a result, it has "taken on a different character than originally anticipated," Maryann says. Rather than simply being used for storage, it has become a more public space.

Silver Coast also has a high-ceilinged art gallery that displays the work of local artists. Maryann convinced one of her best friends from high school, Justine Ferrari, who owned an art gallery, to become the winery's curator and choose all the work. In fact, Silver Coast showcases art not only on its walls, but also on its bottles.

For the labels, Maryann decided to sponsor a contest. When she took out ads in the local newspaper, she expected to get approximately 60 entries, but she didn't anticipate the way the word would spread. Retired grandparents told their children. Vacationers took the ads home with them. By the deadline, Maryann had received more than 380 entries from all over the nation. She laughs, "My children didn't get Christmas presents," since the contest took up so much time. Although it was a difficult decision because "there were so many wonderful labels," she managed to narrow it down to 10 artists. The winners were exhibited at Justine's gallery, and their work appeared on the initial Silver Coast offerings. Maryann intended to use new designs every year, but she discovered that she liked the labels too much to change them so frequently. Instead, there will be a different label for each varietal.

Eventually, Silver Coast plans to hire a full-time winemaker, but it has relied on consultants during its first years. The winery has planted about eight acres of muscadines, from which it will make some wines. But since the area is unsuitable for vinifera, it buys the majority of its grapes from regional farmers. Currently, it produces approximately 5,500 cases a year. In the future, Maryann hopes to reach a 10,000-case capacity. She doesn't expect to expand beyond that because, she notes wryly, "I still have a family, and I like them."

In discussing Silver Coast, Maryann says, "I'm very lucky that my family is involved because that gives it the ability to work." She laughs that her new career means her husband has had to continue in his old one. John, an orthopedic surgeon, always said that he would retire at a certain age. Maryann explains that when they started Silver Coast, he was past that age, but "I said, 'Honey, you have to keep cutting. One of us has to have an income.' " John has been studying winemaking and would eventually like to join the winery staff full-time. Maryann jokes, "I told him that we could just set him up a little office where he could be the orthopedist resident."

Maryann's children help at Silver Coast as well, especially during events. She notes that the favorite task of Gabriel, her six-year-old son, is moving barrels because he "feels really empowered with the pallet jack." She admits that, at first, "I was a little nervous, but he really practiced and got to the point where he could actually maneuver the barrels better than I could by the end of the day." He also helps with other tasks. When the tanks were delivered, she and Gabriel cleaned them. To get rid of a particularly tough patch of tartrate, she mixed a baking-soda paste and told him, "Okay, Gabriel, now we have to use some elbow grease." He picked up the paste and asked, "Mom, is this the elbow grease?" Maryann says, "It was so precious. He was so sincere. I had to spend the next 10 minutes explaining what elbow grease was."

Maryann feels good about what she has accomplished at Silver Coast. She likes the winery's physical elements, such as the ceiling lights from a renovated Baptist church, but she insists that what gives her the most satisfaction is "the reception of our customers." She says, "It was always my concept that in southeastern North Carolina, this would be considered 'our winery' by all the people who live here." She envisioned people asking, "Have you seen our winery?" This, she notes with pride, "seems to be happening." Guy Ferrari, Justine's husband, who also works at the winery, suggests one reason why. He says, "It's amazing to come down that dirt road. You don't know what you're going to see, and it's like the curtain comes up. It's a wonderful place."

Silver Coast Winery Wine List

 Whites
Chardonnay, Seyval Blanc

 Rosé
Silver Coast Rosé

Reds
Barbera, Cabernet Sauvignon, Merlot

Recommend Pairings from Silver Coast Winery

Seyval Blanc with spicy shrimp or fresh strawberries and pineapples

Chardonnay with bruschetta or oily fish such as king mackerel or salmon with a horseradish crust

Silver Coast Winery

Profile: Albert Gomes, Tasting-room Staff, Silver Coast Winery

Albert Gomes

At five years old, Albert Gomes began helping his father make wine. By the time he was 10, they would go together to the local train station to taste grapes in the boxcars. There, Gomes learned about grapes' properties, such as skin, color, and flavor. He says, "My father was a master. Everything I learned about wine, I really learned from him. That was 40 years of winemaking experience, being at his side."

His father was born in the United States. During the Depression, he was raised in Portugal, where his family owned hundreds of acres of vineyards. His uncles and aunts taught him the business. When he returned to the States, he made 250 gallons of wine and five gallons of vinegar each year. He shared his hobby and passion with his son. The two made wine together until 1992, when Albert Gomes, Sr., passed away. In the next couple of years, his son made a few more batches, then stopped. He hasn't made wine since 1997.

In 2001, Albert Gomes's life changed again. After 35 years as an educator, he retired, and he and his wife moved from Connecticut to North Carolina. They had started looking for a place 18 years earlier. Gomes laughs, "I'm a little compulsive about planning ahead." After exploring communities up and down the eastern seaboard and in Hawaii, the Virgin Islands, Barbados, and the Caribbean, they "fell in love" with the North Carolina coast. They found a residence they liked, but there was a problem: their old house had an ideal basement for storing wine, but the new one didn't. So, in preparation for the move, "we had two and a half years to drink 500 bottles of wine," Gomes says. "Such a problem." The cellar had "some great vintages," including wines that were 30 and 40 years old that Gomes had made with his father. Drinking them was bittersweet. He enjoyed them, and he looked forward to his new life, but when the cellar was gone, it seemed to signal the end of his involvement with wine.

Within months of retiring, Gomes realized he was bored. He began looking for part-time work. Intrigued by the nearby construction of Silver Coast Winery, he applied for a job. The owner, Maryann Azzato, not only hired him for the tasting room but eventually convinced him to work 40-hour weeks and to offer wine-tasting classes on Saturdays.

Gomes enjoys his new career, and he still considers himself an educator. His goal is for people to enjoy learning about wines. He remembers some of his own experiences. In his early 20s, he took trips to New York City and went to the Rainbow Room, where the wine list was as thick as a book. He loved paging through the selections: "It was an amazing experience for me. There were wines that I had only heard about listed there. I'm sure that I annoyed the waiters because I took so much time, but the whole wine-selection experience was great." This is his ideal: "If we can help people with their wine selections, and help educate them about wines, that's great."

For Gomes, working at Silver Coast is more than something to do. It offers a bridge to the past. The smell of the winery's barrel room reminds him of his father's basement, which had five 50-gallon oak casks and strings of onions, garlic, and salted hams. To tasting-room visitors, Gomes passes along information that he learned at his father's side. He has become interested in making wine again. One day, he brought a framed photograph of his father and put it on a shelf near the tasting bar. "It puts me in touch with him," Gomes explains.

$\mathcal{A}$lphabetical List of Wineries

Bennett Vineyards (1993)
Biltmore Estate Winery (1977)
Cerminaro Vineyard (2001)
Chateau Laurinda (1997)
Chatham Hill Winery (1999)
Dennis Vineyards (1997)
Duplin Wine Cellars (1976)
Germanton Vineyard and Winery (1981)
Hanover Park Vineyard (1999)
Hinnant Family Vineyard (2002)*
Martin Vineyards (1993)
Moonrise Bay Vineyard (2000)
RagApple Lassie Vineyards (2002)
RayLen Vineyards (2000)
Ritler Ridge Vineyards (2000)
Rockhouse Vineyards (1998)
Shelton Vineyards (2000)
SilkHope Winery (2000)
Silver Coast Winery (2002)
Stony Mountain Vineyards (2002)*
The Teensy Winery (1986)
Thistle Meadow Winery (2002)*
Waldensian Heritage Wines (1989)
Westbend Vineyards (1988)
Windy Gap Vineyards (2000)

*See Appendix 2: New Wineries

New Wineries

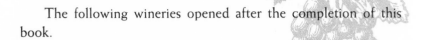

The following wineries opened after the completion of this book.

Hinnant Family Vineyard

826 Pine Level-Micro Road
Pine Level, N.C. 27568
Phone: 919-965-3350
E-mail: hinnant@goldsboro.net
Hours: Tuesday-Sunday, noon-6 P.M.

Owners: R. Willard Hinnant and Bob Hinnant
Winemaker: Bob Hinnant

Directions: From U.S. 70, exit north on Peedin Road. Travel straight for approximately 3 miles. The vineyard is on the right. From Interstate 95, take Exit 97 to U.S. 70 East. Travel approximately 3 miles to the second stoplight, then turn left on Peedin Road. Travel straight for approximately 3 miles. The vineyard is on the right.

Hinnant Family Vineyard Wine List
muscadine wines

Stony Mountain Vineyards
(open for visitors in May 2003)

26370 Mountain Ridge Road
Albemarle, N.C. 28001
Phone: 704-982-0922
E-mail: stonymtn@vnet.net

Owner: Ken Furr

Directions: From Albemarle, drive east on N.C. 24/27 for 3 miles, turn left at the Stone Mountain sign, and then turn right on Mountain Ridge Road. The winery is on the right after 0.9 mile.

Stony Mountain Vineyards Wine List
Chardonnay, Cabernet Sauvignon, Merlot, Syrah, Pinot Gris

Thistle Meadow Winery

102 Thistle Meadows
Laurel Springs, N.C. 28644
Phone: 800-233-1505
E-mail: tom@grapestompers.com
Hours: Monday-Saturday, 10 A.M.-4 P.M.

Owner: Tom Burgiss
Winemaker: Tom Burgiss

Directions: If you're traveling north on the Blue Ridge Parkway, go less than 0.1 mile past Milepost 246 to Elkknob Road. Follow Elkknob Road for 3 miles. You'll see signs on the left at the top of the drive. If you're traveling south on the parkway, go past Milepost 247 and look for Elkknob Road. From Interstate 77, take U.S. 421 North toward North Wilkesboro. At North Wilkesboro, go north on N.C. 18. You will reach a junction where Elkknob Road is on the right and N.C. 13 is on the left. Turn on to Elkknob Road. The winery is the first drive.

Thistle Meadow Winery Wine List
a variety of wines made from concentrate

$\mathcal{U}$seful Resources

There are an enormous number of books, websites, and other resources for those interested in wine. We list only a small selection here.

Books of Interest

Adams, Leon D. *The Wines of America*. 4th ed. Boston: Houghton Mifflin, 1990.

Gohdes, Clarence. *Scuppernong: North Carolina's Grape and Its Wines*. Durham: Duke University Press, 1982.

Jones, H. G., ed. *Sketches in North Carolina USA, 1872 to 1878: Vineyard Scenes by Mortimer O. Heath*. Chapel Hill: North Carolina Society Imprints, 2001.

Lukacs, Paul. *American Vintage: From Isolation to International Renown— The Rise of American Wine*. Boston: Houghton Mifflin, 2000.

Morton, Lucie T. *Winegrowing in Eastern America: An Illustrated Guide to Viniculture East of the Rockies*. Ithaca, N.Y.: Cornell University Press, 1985.

Robinson, Jancis, ed. *Jancis Robinson's Concise Wine Companion*. Oxford: Oxford University Press, 2001.

Periodicals of Interest

On the Vine
Wine East
The Wine Report

Websites of Interest

www.ncwine.org
www.allamericanwineries.com
www.carolinawinecountry.com
www.southernvine.com/index.htm
www.wine-lovers-page.com
www.tarheelwines.com
www.travelenvoy.com/wine.htm
www.visitnc.com
www.wineeducation.org
www.wineandcuisine.org
www.grapestompers.com
www.freethegrapes.org

Organizations of Interest

American Wine Society
North Carolina Grape Council
North Carolina Muscadine Grape Growers Association
North Carolina Winegrower's Association

Index

North Carolina Grape Council,
    45, 78, 164
North Carolina State University,
    164, 168
North Carolina Wine Growers
    Associatioin, 45, 137

Old North State Winegrowers
    Cooperative, 112-13, 131
Olmsted, Frederick Law, 24
On the Vine, 79-80

Parducci Winery, 122
Parker, Robert, 143-44
Pierce's disease, 138-39, 168
Powell, Dennis, 64
Preston, Tommy, 104
Prohibition, 1, 9, 109, 158

Raffaldini Vineyards, 2, 79
RagApple Lassie Vineyards, 114-
    20, 131
Raleigh, Walter, 6
Ravenswood, 78
RayLen Vineyards, 12, 19, 20,
    103, 116, 121-127, 131, 134-
    35
Reed, David, 136-37
Rigby, Stephen, 140
Ritler Ridge Vineyards, 45-50
Ritz, Tim, 46-50
Rockhouse Vineyards, 51-57
Rooster Ridge Vineyards, 112
Round Peak Vineyards, 121-22

Schwab, Ed, 107
Shelton, Charlie, 128-32, 134

Shelton, Ed, 128-32, 134
Shelton Vineyards, 18, 103, 115,
    123, 128-35, 180
Shepard, Steve, 12, 16-17, 19, 20,
    107, 116, 121-24, 126-27, 143
SilkHope Winery, 136-39
Silver Coast Winery, 2, 178-85
Silver Creek Vineyards, 20, 44-45,
    123, 131
Simmers, Gary, 58-59
Simpson, David, 98-104
Simpson, Judy, 98-104
Smith, Fleet, 172
Snyder, Gary, 115
Southland Estate Winery, 159
Stony Mountain Vineyards, 189-
    90
Surry Community College, 12,
    131, 148-49, 164

Tabor Hill Vineyards, 44
Teensy Winery, The, 2, 14, 60-63,
    164
Thistle Meadow Winery, 190
Thomer, Marilyn, 122
Thornton, Robert, 152
Tongo, Joseph, 8
Trottier, Arthur, 176
Troxell, Ray, 123, 129, 131, 134-
    35

University of California at Davis,
    129, 174

Vanderbilt, George Washington,
    23